REVISION GUIDE

History for CCEA GCSE

Third Edition

Finbar Madden

HODDER EDUCATION
AN HACHETTE UK COMPANY

The Publishers would like to thank the following for permission to reproduce copyright material.

Photo credits

Photo credits p. xii © Bettmann/Corbis

Acknowledgements

The following questions are © CCEA 2015, reprinted with the permission of the Northern Ireland Council for the Curriculum, Examinations and Assessment: p. ix taken from pp. 189–193 Paper 1 Option 5 Changing Relationships: Britain, Northern Ireland and the Republic of Ireland 1965–85 11(a) (i), (ii), (b), (c); p. x taken from p. 70 Paper 2 Section A 1(a), (b).

Orders: please contact Bookpoint Ltd, Park Drive, 130 Milton Park, Abingdon, Oxon OX14 4SE. Telephone: (44) 01235 827720. Fax: (44) 01235 400454. Email education@bookpoint.co.uk Lines are open from 9 a.m. to 5 p.m., Monday to Saturday, with a 24-hour message answering service. You can also order through our website: www.hoddereducation.co.uk

ISBN: 978 1 4718 4463 8

First published in 2007
Second edition published in 2011
This edition published in 2015 by
Hodder Education,
An Hachette UK Company
Carmelite House
50 Victoria Embankment
London EC4Y 0DZ
www.hoddereducation.co.uk

Impression number 10 9 8 7 6 5 4 3 2
Year 2019 2018 2017 2016

Cover photo © akg-images; PETER KEMP/AP/Press Association Images; MPI/Hulton Archive/Getty Images
Typeset by Aptara Inc.
Printed in India
A catalogue record for this title is available from the British Library.

CONTENTS

Introduction

ABOUT THE BOOK

Welcome to *History for CCEA GCSE Revision Guide*. This book has been written to help you achieve the best mark possible in your GCSE History examination. However, before we start looking at the specifics of GCSE History in detail, let's see if you can answer the following (simple) question:

What are the two most basic things that you need to have to pass any examination?

No, it's not a trick question! If you hope to pass an exam, no matter what the subject, you need:

(a) knowledge of the facts
(b) the skills that will allow you to use your knowledge to answer the questions asked.

It's as simple – and as difficult – as that!

This book aims to make it as simple as possible by focusing on these key elements in the context of GCSE History. It hopes to prepare you in two ways:

1 Firstly, and most basically, it sets out the essential facts that you need to know to be able to answer the questions set. There's no way around it – you need to know this stuff!

2 Secondly, and equally importantly, it provides you with guidance on how to acquire and develop the examination skills that will enable you to achieve your full potential in the examination.

The book covers four topics:

- Germany 1918–1939
- Peace, War and Neutrality: Britain, Northern Ireland and Ireland 1932–1949
- Changing Relationships: Britain, Northern Ireland and Ireland 1965–1985
- The Cold War 1945–1991

Each topic covered is divided into units. Each unit is then divided into appropriate sub-sections, designed to break up the knowledge content into easy to manage pieces. Each sub-section contains a summary of the key facts relevant to that part of the course as well as a number of simple revision tasks. As you read through and come to grips with the facts, you should find that completing these tasks will:

1 enable to you to understand the facts more fully

2 provide you with easy-to-remember revision tables and diagrams.

All the way through the text you'll find words and phrases highlighted in bold. These are examples of the kind of subject-specific language that you can expect to come across in some parts of the examination and whose correct use will undoubtedly impress the examiners. You will find these words defined in the glossary at the back of the book. However, before you look them up, try and work out their meanings for yourself.

GETTING YOUR REVISION RIGHT

This chapter focuses in particular on outlining and developing the skills that will enable you to approach the examination with confidence. You'll find information on the course structure and an overview of how the examination is organised. You'll also find suggestions on how to approach revision. Most importantly, you'll find practical information on sitting the examination. This includes guidelines on how much time you should spend on each question and suggestions about how to deal with the specific question styles that are used by the examiners.

STRUCTURE OF THE COURSE

The course comprises three units. These are:

- Studies in Depth (Unit 1)
- Outline Study (Unit 2)
- Investigative Study (Unit 3).

Unit 1

In Unit 1 you must study **two** Studies in Depth.

One Study in Depth should be one of the following options:

- Option 1: Germany 1918–1939; or
- Option 2: Russia c.1916–1939 (not covered in this book); or
- Option 3: United States of America c.1920–1941 (not covered in this book).

The other Study in Depth should be one of the following options:

- Option 4: Peace, War and Neutrality: Britain, Northern Ireland and Ireland 1932–1949; or
- Option 5: Changing Relationships: Britain, Northern Ireland and Ireland 1965–1985.

Unit 2

In Unit 2 you must study the following Outline Study:

- The Cold War 1945–1991.

Unit 3

The Investigative Study is taken as a controlled assessment and is not covered in this book.

If you want a detailed breakdown of the CCEA GCSE History specification, you can download it from the CCEA History Microsite at www.ccea.org.uk/history.

ASSESSMENT OBJECTIVES

The assessment objectives for CCEA GCSE History are laid out in detail in the specification. Briefly, there are three assessment objectives that focus on the knowledge, skills and abilities that the examiners assess. The assessment objectives are shown in the box below:

Candidates must demonstrate their ability to:

AO1: recall, select, organise and communicate knowledge and understanding of history;
AO2: demonstrate their understanding of the past through explanation and analysis of:
- key concepts: causation, consequence, continuity, change and significance within an historical context; and
- key features and characteristics of the periods studied and the relationships between them; and

AO3: understand, analyse and evaluate:
- source material as part of an historical enquiry; and
- how aspects of the past have been interpreted and represented in different ways as part of an historical enquiry.

THE EXAMINATION

There are two papers in the examination. Paper 1 covers the Studies in Depth while Paper 2 focuses on the Outline Study.

The layout of the papers is reasonably straightforward. To start off, make sure that you are doing the right sections on the day of the exam – it *has* been known for people to get it wrong! You have some choice of questions to answer in Section A of Paper 1 and some choice with regard to the essay in Section B of Paper 2. Before deciding which questions to do in these sections, glance over all questions quickly, noting any areas where you feel particularly strong (or weak). Then, on the basis of this, make your question choice and stick with it!

You can access past papers on the CCEA History Microsite at www.ccea.org.uk/history. Here's how they break down:

Paper 1

- Lasts 2 hours.
- Is worth 50 per cent of the entire GCSE.
- You must answer two questions from a choice of three on **either** Germany **or** Russia **or** USA and all questions on either Britain, Northern Ireland and Ireland 1932–1949 or Britain, Northern Ireland and Ireland 1965–1985.
- Each question is broken down into parts which include short answer questions and questions requiring extended writing.
- Some of the questions on Britain, Northern Ireland and Ireland 1932–1949 and Britain, Northern Ireland and Ireland 1965–1985 make use of source materials as a stimulus for your thinking.

Paper 2

- Lasts 1 hour 15 minutes.
- Is worth 25 per cent of the entire GCSE.
- Questions only on the Cold War.
- Includes one four-part source-based question in Section A and one essay question from a choice of two in Section B.

TIMING

Getting the timing right in the examination is crucial. You should spend **no more** than the amount of time suggested below on each question part.

Indeed, if possible in Paper 1 try and gain a little extra time in the questions worth fewer marks to use on the more valuable questions. If you run out of time on those questions then you run the risk of losing a lot of marks. This could have a major impact on your overall grade.

Similarly in Paper 2 spend **no more** than the indicated amount of time on each section. There are too many marks at stake for you to leave yourself short of time when it comes to Question 1 (d) and the essay question that you choose to do in Section B.

Paper 1

Answer two questions (from a choice of three) from your chosen topic in Section A. Answer all questions from your chosen topic in Section B.		
SECTION A (answering TWO questions)	**Marks (per question)**	**Timing (per question)**
Question (a)	4 marks	5 minutes
Question (b)	6 marks	7 minutes
Question (c)	15 marks	18 minutes
SECTION B	**Marks**	**Timing**
Question (a) (i)	6 marks	7 minutes
Question (a) (ii)	9 marks	11 minutes
Question (a) (iii)	12 marks	14 minutes
Question (b)	6 marks	7 minutes
Question (c)	17 marks (plus 5 marks for SPaG)	21 minutes

Paper 2

Two Sections (do **BOTH**)		
10 minutes to read sources		
SECTION A Four-part, source-based question	**Marks**	**Timing**
Question 1 (a)	4 marks	5 minutes
Question 1 (b)	6 marks	8 minutes
Question 1 (c)	9 marks	12 minutes
Question 1 (d)	15 marks	19 minutes
SECTION B ONE essay from a choice of TWO	**Marks**	**Timing**
Question 2 **or** 3	16 marks (plus 5 marks for SPaG)	21 minutes

REVISION TECHNIQUES

Everyone revises differently. For some people it is a matter of sitting at a desk; for others pacing up and down. While some people can work with music in the background, others require total silence. The bottom line is, there's no single best way!

Whatever your style, there are a number of practical suggestions as to how you should approach revision and use your time:

- Start your revision in plenty of time.
- Organise a revision timetable for each section of the course.
- Draw up a revision checklist that allows you to focus on the parts of the course that you are most concerned about.
- Set yourself a target of material to cover in each session – for example, the impact of the Wall Street Crash – and stick to it.
- Revise for short periods – 15–20 minutes, for example – and take breaks in between.
- Use the Activities after each section as a way of testing your grasp of the key facts.
- Review what you have covered at the end of the day and again the next day to make sure you have internalised the information.
- Be open to using a range of ways of remembering material. For example, rhymes, mnemonics, coding and diagrams.
- Practise questions from past papers to familiarise yourself with the kinds of questions that the examiners set.
- Consult CCEA Mark Schemes and Chief Examiner's Reports to see what the examiners are looking for and – more importantly – the mistakes that they want you to avoid.
- Leave yourself time to revisit material that you have already revised closer to the time of the examination.

SITTING THE EXAMINATION

General Points

- Make sure you're **looking at the right question**. This is particularly relevant to the two Northern Ireland sections in Paper 1.
- Look for **all of the questions** – some may be over the page. Don't forget to check!
- Follow the **instructions** on the front of the exam paper and within each section.
- **Read** each question carefully and slowly – more than once. Take the time to understand just what you are being asked.
- Use a highlighter pen to emphasise **key points** in a question.
- Keep your answer relevant. Answer the question that has been set – not the one you wish had been set! That is what you'll be marked on.
- Remember the connection between the amount of marks for each question and how much you are expected to write (see above).
- Stick rigidly to whatever dates are given in a question. You will get no marks for going beyond the dates given.
- If you want to score strongly in each part of the examination, you must spend the appropriate amount of time on each question. Too much time spent on one section will mean too little left for others and will cost you significant amounts of marks.
- Stay for the **full amount** of time. You can't get marks if you're not there!

PAPER 1

- Paper 1 includes two types of questions, one of which asks you to use historical sources.
- Your answers must demonstrate a detailed **knowledge**. This book provides you with the **key facts** on each topic. Learn these thoroughly!
- Structure your answer. Most frequently a **chronological framework** will be the best way to achieve this.
- Select appropriate **facts** to answer the question asked.
- Many pupils lose marks by **failing to identify all relevant information**. Instead of writing a lot about one point, try to write less about a number of points.
- You need to demonstrate your mastery of the appropriate historical skills.

This is a **how** or **why** question and the examiners are looking for you to answer it in a **logical** and **focused manner**. You should be aiming to write a paragraph. A good way to approach this question is **chronologically**.

Paper 1 OPTION 1: Germany 1918–1939

This question is on Key Issue 1: The Aftermath of the First World War and the Weimar Republic

1 (a) Describe two terms of the Treaty of Versailles. [4]

(b) How did Hitler try to increase support for the Nazi Party following his release from prison? [6]

(c) Explain how the Weimar governments dealt with problems between 1929 and 1933. In your answer refer to the bullet points and use other relevant knowledge.

- Political problems
- Economic problems [15]

This type of question **does not require explanation**, but a recall of knowledge. Write one detailed sentence on each point.

This type of question – asking **how/why** or **how and why** - requires both **analysis** and **explanation**. When you are asked 'how', you should provide an explanation. When asked 'why', you need to give the **reasons** for an event or decision.

You must make sure that you focus on **both bullet points** in your answer. Too many students focus only on one and lose a lot of marks. Remember, though, you may not need to write an equal amount on each bullet point.

It is important that you answer the question by using each of the bullet points provided in the question and writing an appropriately detailed answer on each. Make sure you refer back to the question.

These bullet points are designed as **prompts**; you need to **develop** these bullet points by using your own knowledge. You should also include other relevant knowledge where possible.

Here you are using the given source and your knowledge to **describe** an event. You should aim to write about 5–6 sentences in total.

In this answer the examiner will expect you to reach a **judgement** about an event, again using the source and your own knowledge. You should be using phrases such as 'I agree…' or 'I disagree…'. The most important thing is to remember to give your own **viewpoint**.

Paper 1 OPTION 5: Changing Relationships: Britain, Northern Ireland and the Republic of Ireland 1965–1985

Answer all questions

11(a) (i) **Study Source A**

Using Source A, and your own knowledge, describe O'Neill's plans to improve the economy of Northern Ireland. [6]

(ii) **Study Source B**

Using Source B, and your own knowledge, explain the main demands of the Northern Ireland Civil Rights Association (NICRA). [9]

(iii) **Study Source C**

Source C suggests that British troops ended up carrying out policing duties in Northern Ireland. Do you agree with the view that the only reason for the introduction of British troops to Northern Ireland was to do the job of the RUC?

Explain your answer using Source C and your own knowledge. [12]

(b) In what ways did the people of Northern Ireland react to the Hunger Strikes of 1980 and 1981? [6]

(c) How effective was internment in dealing with the political situation in Northern Ireland in the 1970s? [17] and [SPaG 5]

Here you are using the source and your knowledge to **explain** an event. You should aim to write about 7–8 sentences, developing your answer a little more.

This question is asking you to **explain** past events. Remember, there is no source this time. You must use the source and your own knowledge to make your point. To show that you know the topic, include relevant detail. There are fewer marks available here than for the previous answer, so keep an eye on your timing!

Given the amount of marks available, this should be your **longest answer**. Remember that there are also five additional marks available for your use of spelling, punctuation and grammar, so try your best to get them! You need to show the examiner the extent to which you **agree** or **disagree** with the statement in the question. Try to give your answer an essay-like structure. Introduce the issue, give your arguments for and against and finish off with your own **views**.

PAPER 2

Section A: Source Question

- Read the sources and the source questions carefully. Use a highlighter pen to underline **key points**.
- Identify all **relevant information** in the sources.
- Ask yourself whether or not the source is providing you with **fact** or **opinion**.
- Use your **own knowledge** to explain the **background** to the source. This will help you determine its **reliability**.
- Remember to consider what the source **fails to say** as much as what it does – again, your own knowledge will be essential here.
- The **reliability** and **bias** of sources must be considered.
- Use the **sources** (whatever ones are specified) in your answers to support what you say when you are instructed to.
- Use your **own knowledge** in your answers to support what you say when you are instructed to.
- As with Paper 1, look for a **number of different points** in your answer. Frequently the examiner will award a mark for each point mentioned up to the maximum available.

Here the examiners are looking for you to provide approximately **FOUR** pieces of information from the indicated source that tell you something about the focus of the question.

Remember that this is a **straightforward comprehension question** that requires you to provide **no contextual/ background knowledge**.

You don't need to write more than a paragraph to answer this type of question. Spending too long will not gain you any more marks and will lose you valuable time for where you need it most.

Paper 2 Section A

Answer **all** of this section.

1 This question is about the spread of communist control in Eastern Europe after the Second World War.

(a) **Study Source A.**

What does Source A tell us about why the USSR spread communism to the countries of Eastern Europe after the Second World War? [4]

(b) **Study Sources A and B**

How far does Source B support the view in Source A about the actions of Stalin and the USSR after the Second World War? [6]

(c) **Study Source C.**

How useful is Source C in telling us how the West reacted following the Soviet invasion of Hungary? [9]

(d) 'The USSR had to keep control over Eastern Europe for its own safety'.

Using Sources A, B, C and D, and your own knowledge, explain whether you agree with this interpretation of the actions and policies of the USSR in Eastern Europe after the Second World War. [15]

This question asks you to use **two sources**. It can be awkward if you don't **structure your answer carefully**. The first thing to do is **identify the relevant points** in the first source and then **look for similar points in the second source** (i.e. where they **agree**). However, if you want to aim for top marks you must also **indicate the areas where the two sources do NOT agree**. You should identify these points as you go through each source.

This is the kind of question that can cause a lot of problems. Remember that you are being asked to consider **TWO** things:

1. How **RELIABLE** the source is.

   Reliability means **whether or not we can take what it says to be true**. Keep in mind issues such as the source's **type**, its **author, when** it was written, **who** it was written for (its **audience**), **why** it was written (**motive**) and its **tone and content**.

   When discussing reliability the issue of **bias** will more than likely appear. Remember, just because a source is **biased** – and all sources are biased in some way or other – does not mean that it is not useful. **ALL sources are useful for what they tell us about how a person or group was thinking**.

2. How **USEFUL** the source is.

   Useful means **what do you learn from the source**, what does it tell us about the event in question? Most importantly, remember to comment – considering your own knowledge – on what the source does **NOT** tell us (its **limitations**).

Remember, you must cover **BOTH** reliability and utility if you want to gain top marks.

The key point here is to remember to **use BOTH the sources** (**ALL** of them!) **AND your own knowledge** to help you make a **judgement** about **how an event has been interpreted**. The amount of marks available mean that your answer should be a mini-essay.

First of all the sources will more than likely present you with **a range of interpretations** about an event. You need to be able to **identify these different viewpoints and explain why they are different**. It is your **own knowledge** that will enable you to judge whether or not the interpretation given in the question is right or wrong. Make sure that your answer **reflects these different viewpoints**. In the end, remember to **come to a conclusion**!

HOW TO APPROACH SOURCES

As you look at the different kinds of sources you might encounter, consider some of the following ideas to try and improve the quality of your answer.

Written sources

Primary sources

A primary source is one that dates from the time of the event.

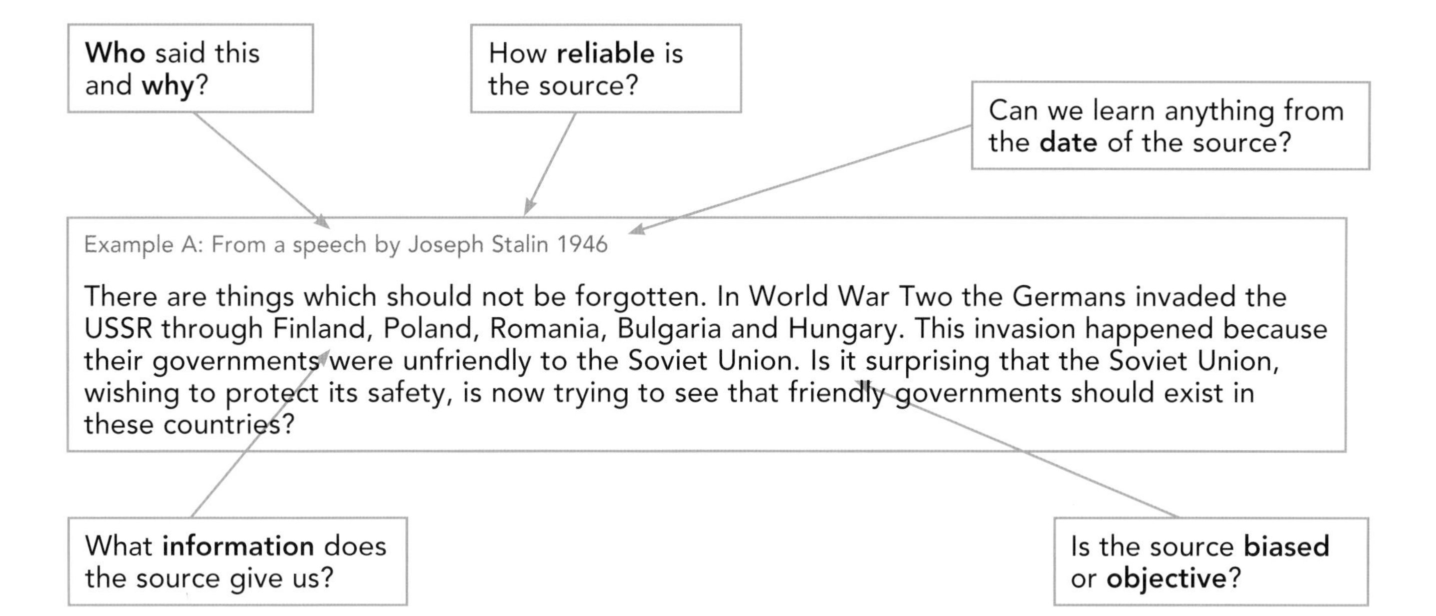

Secondary sources

A secondary source usually comes from a time after the event being written about, such as historians' accounts.

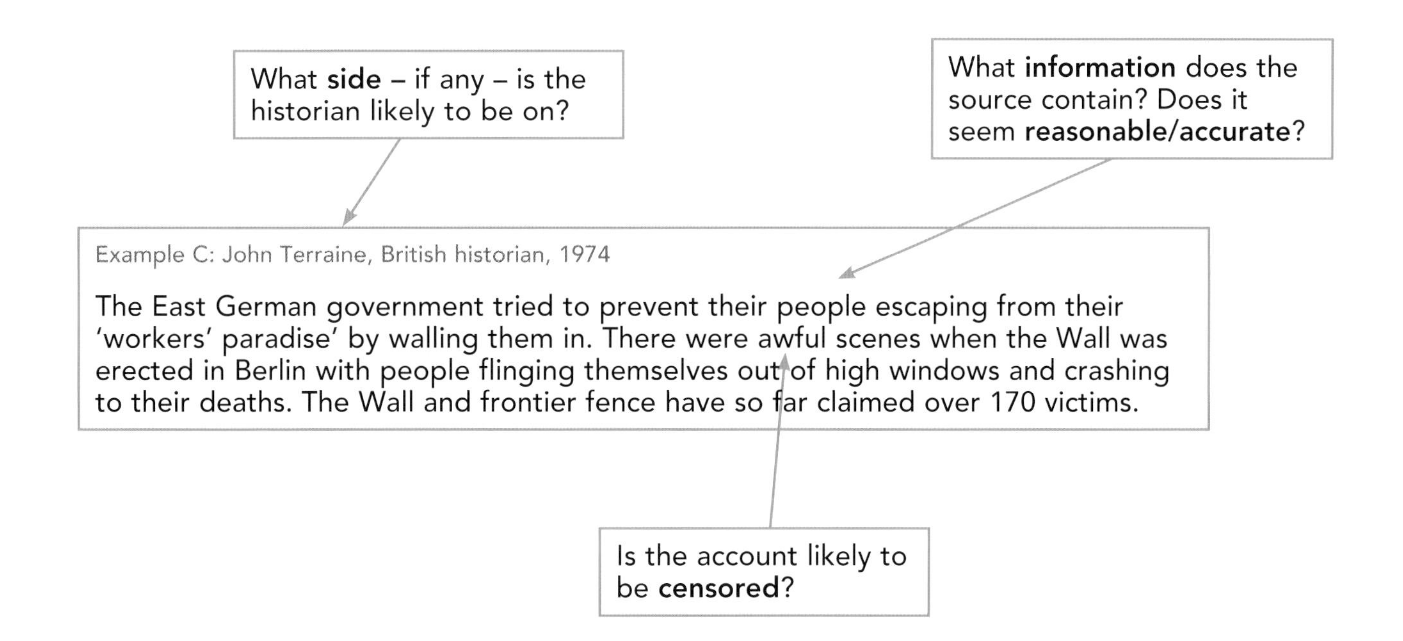

Photographic evidence

We expect photographs to be reliable, but this is not always the case. When you get a photograph as a source you should ask yourself the following questions about it.

Example F: Photograph taken in Prague in 1968

Is the photograph **genuine** or **faked**?

Which **side** is the photographer on? What does the photograph tell us?

Is the photograph **propaganda**? Is it **biased**?

Czechs shout abuse at Soviet troops sitting on top of a tank, Prague 1968

Can we trust the caption?

Does the photograph **tell us everything** about the situation? Does it tell us what happened just before, or after this photograph was taken? Does this tell us how **ALL** Czechs felt? Were other Czechs cheering the Russian soldiers?

PAPER 2

Section B: Essay Questions

- Look carefully at the question. Make sure you read it all – don't just focus on one word or phrase.
- You will be asked to examine changes in the relations between the USSR and USA over a given number of years.
- **Underline** the key dates and words in the question.
- Spend a few minutes jotting down an essay plan that will take the examiner through the topic in a logical manner.
- **Structure** your answer. Use **paragraphs** (and again most likely a **chronological framework**.
- **Refer to the question frequently** throughout your answer and avoid narrative.
- Put in **relevant information** only. An essay on the development of the Cold War in Europe 1945–68 does not require any analysis of China, Korea, Cuba or Vietnam!
- Remember that you are being asked to **come to a conclusion**, not simply list all of the facts that you think are relevant to the issue.
- Finally, remember that there are also five additional marks available for your use of spelling, punctuation and grammar; make sure you get them all!

Use **key words** from the question to help you structure your answer.

Make sure to cover **all of the areas and issues** mentioned.

Paper 2 Section B

Answer **one** of the following questions.

2 How and why did events in Berlin in the period 1945–1961 cause tensions to develop between the USA and the USSR? [16] and [SPaG 5]

Check the dates that the question requires you to cover. **Do not** go beyond these dates.

There are five additional marks available for spelling, punctuation and grammar. Get them all!

Spend **21 minutes** on the essay question.

Germany 1918–1939

THE AFTERMATH OF THE FIRST WORLD WAR AND THE WEIMAR REPUBLIC

GERMANY IN 1918 (I)

IMPACT OF THE WAR

Initially most Germans welcomed the war but discontent soon emerged due to:

- increasing food and fuel shortages
- a decline in the value of the currency
- an increase in ill health.

Although the people were being told that the war was going well, by October 1918 the government knew that it was lost. Over 6 million soldiers had either been killed or wounded, the most recent military attack had failed, Germany's allies (Austria–Hungary, Bulgaria and Turkey) were close to defeat, the army was exhausted and troops were deserting.

In late October 1918, therefore, the **Kaiser** was persuaded to make Germany into a **constitutional monarchy**. This was because:

- There was growing unrest among Germany's working classes which might lead to revolution.
- It was felt that a civilian government would obtain fairer peace terms.
- It was believed that the new government would get the blame for ending the war. Therefore the army could accuse it of stabbing them in the back.

As a result Prince Max of Baden became Germany's new **Chancellor**.

WHAT YOU NEED TO KNOW

You need to understand **how** and **why** Germans' attitudes to the war changed and **how** this impacted on the Kaiser.

ACTIVITY

Make notes under the following headings:

- The impact of the war at home
- The changes made to the government
- Why these changes were made

GERMANY IN 1918 (II)

ABDICATION

These concessions were not enough for those who wanted Germany made into a **republic**. On 3 November 1918, a revolt broke out at Kiel and Wilhelmshaven naval bases. Local workers joined in and the protests spread across Germany with Russian-style workers' councils (Soviets) being set up. Within a week Berlin had been brought to a standstill by a general strike while socialist republics had been set up in Bavaria and Saxony.

With Germany facing revolution the Kaiser was persuaded to **abdicate**. He did so on 9 November 1918. At the same time Prince Max was replaced by Social Democratic Party (SDP) leader, Friedrich Ebert. Ebert soon made the following crucial decisions:

- He set up a new government and declared Germany a republic.
- He made a deal with the head of the army, General Wilhelm Groener. By this he agreed to maintain the power of the army, **judiciary** and **civil service** and resist the growth of **communism**. Groener agreed to support the new government.

WHAT YOU NEED TO KNOW

You need to know **why** the Kaiser left and **how** people reacted. Make sure that you are clear about all of the changes that took place.

ACTIVITY

1 Match the date to the event:

Date	Event
3/11/18	Germany declared a republic ....
9/11/18	Naval revolt ....
11/11/18	Ebert becomes leader of Germany ....
	Kaiser abdicates ....

- On 11 November 1918, Germany signed an **armistice** ending the fighting in the war.

These events shocked most ordinary Germans who had been led to believe that the war was going well. Their anger was directed towards the new government – just as the Kaiser and army had wanted.

THREATS FROM THE LEFT

THE SPARTACISTS

Ebert faced particular opposition from the **left-wing** Spartacists, led by Rosa Luxemburg and Karl Liebknecht. They believed that Germany should be run by Soviets, not by the ***Reichstag*** as Ebert wanted. On 6 January 1919 the Spartacists – now calling themselves the German Communist Party (KPD) – launched a *putsch* (rising) against the new government.

The *putsch* was crushed by the army supported by the Free Corps, a **right-wing** volunteer army mainly comprising anti-communist ex-soldiers. By 15 January 1919 the rising was over and both Spartacist leaders and many of their followers had been murdered. The whole episode created long-term division between the SPD and KPD which prevented them from ever co-operating together against the right-wing.

FURTHER UNREST

Over the next few months the left wing posed further challenges. In March 1919:

- Berlin was the scene of further communist unrest. Again the Free Corps was called upon to act; again they destroyed the opposition.
- A Communist Republic was declared in Bavaria. The government responded by besieging Munich, the state capital, finally taking back control on 1 May.

ESTABLISHING A NEW SYSTEM

A NEW CONSTITUTION

Elections for the new German Parliament were held in January 1919. The majority of seats were won by the SPD and so Ebert became President.

The first task was to draw up a **constitution**. As Berlin was too violent the politicians moved to the quieter town of Weimar. Thus Germany became known as the Weimar Republic.

The constitution was accepted by the Parliament on 31 July 1919. It made Germany the most democratic country in the world:

- All citizens (male and female) over the age of 20 could vote.
- Freedom of speech, assembly and movement were guaranteed.
- Freedom of religion was permitted.

However, some parts of the new constitution, which were intended to be strengths, would also turn out to be weaknesses:

Part of constitution	Reason why it was a strength	Reasons why it was a weakness
Proportional Representation (PR) was used for elections (to be held every four years).	This gave all parties the chance of winning seats in parliament.	More parties elected made it harder for anyone to win a majority and allowed parties hostile to Weimar to get elected. This usually meant that governments were made up of a number of parties (**coalitions**) who could fall out quite easily, making laws difficult to pass. This lack of stability – there were 14 different Chancellors between 1919 and 1933 – could undermine democracy.

ACTIVITY

2 Make notes under the following headings:
- Reasons for the Kaiser's abdication
- Why most Germans were shocked by the armistice
- Impact that defeat had on popular attitudes towards Germany's new leaders

WHAT YOU NEED TO KNOW

There were many different political viewpoints in Germany. You need to understand the difference between left and right-wing as well as **how** and **why** some on the left wing wanted to overthrow Ebert's government.

ACTIVITIES

1 Which of the following statements are true or false for the i) SPD and ii) KPD?
- Left-wing party
- Supported **democracy**
- Believed in using violence
- Led by Ebert
- Led by Liebknecht and Luxemburg

2 Give examples of left-wing opposition; include the date, location and outcome.

WHAT YOU NEED TO KNOW

You need to understand **how** the Weimar Constitution worked, **what** its strengths were and – most importantly – **how** its weaknesses might cause problems in the future.

Part of constitution	Reason why it was a strength	Reasons why it was a weakness
In a political crisis, if the government could not get enough support from parliament, Article 48 allowed the President to rule using emergency decrees.	This meant that the country could still be governed even in a crisis.	There was no definition as to what constituted an 'emergency'. Using Article 48 meant that the government was not running the country, which was undemocratic. If Article 48 was used too much and for too long, democracy would be undermined.

In addition, the army, civil service and judiciary remained largely unchanged from the old system. These groups wanted a return to what they saw as the good old days of the Kaiser. Their attitude towards the Weimar Republic remained half-hearted at best and openly hostile at worst.

ACTIVITIES

1 Using the table on this page list the results of the proportional representation and Article 48 parts of the constitution and explain whether they were strengths or weaknesses.

2 Why did it matter that the following groups opposed the Weimar Republic?

- Army
- Civil service
- Judiciary

THE TREATY OF VERSAILLES

TERMS OF THE TREATY

The **Allied** leaders spent early 1919 drawing up the Peace Treaties that would officially end the First World War. The German government expected that the settlement would be based on the ideas of US President Woodrow Wilson. One of his most important ideas concerned self-determination – people's right to decide which country they wanted to live in.

The German delegation was not allowed to take part in the negotiations and did not see the terms of the Treaty until 7 May 1919. At that point they were allowed to make some suggestions, only a few of which were accepted. The final version of the Treaty was published on 16 June. There were three main parts: land, arms and war guilt and **reparations**.

WHAT YOU NEED TO KNOW

The new government was already unpopular because it had ended the war even though it had no choice. Signing the Treaty of Versailles increased its unpopularity. Make sure that you know the Treaty's key terms.

1 Land

- Germany lost territory to France, Belgium and Poland; the latter via the Polish Corridor which **partitioned** the country.
- Germany lost all of her overseas colonies.
- ***Anschluss*** with Austria was forbidden.
- In a number of disputed areas, such as Schleswig, Allenstein, Marienwerder and Silesia, the **Allies** organised **plebiscites** to decide who would govern the regions.

In total Germany lost:

- 13 per cent of its land
- 12 per cent of its population (about 6 million people)
- 15 per cent of its agricultural production
- 48 per cent of its iron production (with similar losses for steel)
- 16 per cent of its coal production.

In addition, all profits from the Saar coalfields were to go to France for fifteen years.

2 Arms

- To stop Germany going to war again, particularly against France, the Rhineland (the area of Germany bordering France) was to be **demilitarised** for 50 kilometres from the border. To ensure that this happened, the area was to be occupied by Allied troops for fifteen years.
- The German army was limited to 100,000 men and **conscription** was prohibited.
- The German navy was limited to 15,000 sailors and six battleships, and no submarines were to be built.
- The creation of a German air force was forbidden.

ACTIVITIES

1 Create a spider diagram listing the key terms of Versailles under the following headings:

- Land
- Military
- War guilt

2 Make notes under the following headings:

- Kind of settlement most Germans were expecting
- How many Germans reacted to the Treaty
- Why it was unfair of Germans to blame the new government for Versailles

3 War guilt and reparations

According to Article 231 of the Treaty, Germany had to admit that it caused the First World War and compensate the Allies for the damage caused during the war by paying reparations. The figure for this would be agreed at a later date.

REACTIONS TO THE TREATY

Many Germans were outraged and christened the Treaty a ***diktat***. They turned on politicians who had signed the armistice (November 1918) that had led to the Treaty. They argued that Germany had been betrayed by these politicians and began calling them 'November Criminals'.

The German government resigned rather than sign the Treaty. However, faced with the threat of renewed war, a new government signed the Treaty in the Palace of Versailles on 28 June 1919.

THREATS FROM THE RIGHT (AND LEFT!)

WHAT YOU NEED TO KNOW

We've already seen the different ways in which the left wing tried to destroy the new Republic. Now it was the turn of the right. What is important for you to understand is **how** the army reacted to the rising.

The left then challenged the government again. What is interesting is **how** the Republic still relied on the unreliable Free Corps to save it.

THE KAPP *PUTSCH*

On 13 March 1920 the Free Corps – led by an extreme **nationalist** journalist and politician Wolfgang Kapp – seized key locations in Berlin. The reason was their anger at the reduction in the size of the army as demanded by the Treaty of Versailles.

Ebert ordered the army to act. However, it refused and the government was forced to flee. Workers in Berlin and elsewhere responded to a call for help from the government and organised a shutdown. Within four days, their strike had brought Berlin to a standstill. With his *putsch* defeated, Kapp fled the country. In its aftermath the Free Corps were broken up but the government took no action against the army.

ASSASSINATIONS

Between 1920 and 1922, 354 murders were carried out by right wingers, including the assassination of Foreign Minister Walter Rathenau in June 1922. The punishments suffered by the perpetrators were usually insignificant. For example, Rathenau's assassins were sentenced on average to four years' imprisonment.

At the same time, those responsible for the 22 murders carried out by the left during these years were usually either given the death sentence or severe punishment by the right-wing legal system.

ACTIVITIES

1. Create a table that shows the reasons, events and results of the Kapp *putsch*.
2. Compare the punishments given to right- and left-wing assassins in these years.
3. Create a table that shows the reasons, events and results of the 'Red Rising'.

'RED RISING'

In 1920 the government faced another threat, this time from workers in the Ruhr who had been on strike in reaction to the Kapp *putsch*. When the *putsch* ended, the communists among the Ruhr's workforce stayed on strike and formed their own **Red Army**. Their aim was to obtain concessions from the government they had just helped save.

This 'Red Rising' was crushed by the army supported by some of the same Free Corps who had just tried to overthrow the government.

THE 1923 ECONOMIC CRISIS

WHAT YOU NEED TO KNOW

The important things to understand here are **why** the crisis developed, how the government responded, **what** it meant for the economy, **how** it affected ordinary Germans and **what** the government did to end it.

REPARATIONS

Long before the 1923 crisis the German economy was in trouble:

- Money had been borrowed to pay for the war and these loans now had to be repaid.
- **Inflation** was growing.
- Germany had lost important industrial and agricultural areas after the Treaty of Versailles.
- The government was borrowing and printing more money.

In January 1921 the situation deteriorated further when the Allies announced that Germany would have to pay £6,600 million in reparations. Germany paid the first instalment; then in December 1922 it announced that it could not afford the next payment and asked for a break.

France refused to agree and, in January 1923, France and Belgium invaded the Ruhr, intending to take what they were owed.

The government ordered the population of the Ruhr to engage in **passive resistance**. This made Germany's economic problems even worse:

- The richest part of the country was not producing anything, thus reducing the country's income.
- Germany had to start importing goods, which cost more money.
- The Ruhr workers still had to be paid, even though they were not working.

Faced with passive resistance, the invading forces killed over 130 people and expelled at least 150,000 Germans from their homes.

HYPERINFLATION

The government's solution to its economic problems was to print even more money and by the autumn of 1923 Germany was experiencing **hyperinflation**. Particularly affected were:

- the poor who had little or nothing
- those living on a fixed income like pensioners
- farmers
- owners of small businesses
- the middle classes whose savings were rendered worthless by hyperinflation.

With money worthless Germany developed into a **barter economy**.

Not everyone suffered. Those whose wealth was not in money were unaffected, while people with debts or mortgages were able to pay off their loans (taken out when money was worth much more) cheaply with the devalued currency.

THE SOLUTION

The crisis resulted in the collapse of the government. In August President Ebert used his powers under Article 48 of the constitution to form a new government led by Gustav Stresemann. Stresemann ended the crisis by:

- ordering an end to passive resistance
- sharply reducing government spending
- agreeing to resume paying reparations, realising that this was the only way to get the French and Belgians out of the Ruhr
- establishing in November 1923 a new national bank, the *Reichsbank*, and introducing a new currency, the Rentenmark.

While Stresemann's actions restored economic stability, the 1923 crisis destroyed the confidence of a significant number of Germans – particularly those in the middle class – in the Weimar Republic.

ACTIVITIES

1 Explain the 1923 crisis using the headings of:
- Reasons
- Results

2 Make a table with two columns under the following headings:
- Groups most affected by the hyperinflation crisis (and reasons why)
- Groups least affected by the hyperinflation crisis (and reasons why)

3 Create a spider diagram illustrating Stresemann's solutions for the 1923 crisis.

RECOVERY

WHAT YOU NEED TO KNOW

Stresemann moved to ensure that Germany stabilised economically and began to get on with her former enemies again. You need to be aware of the agreements he made to achieve this.

In 1924 Stresemann (now Germany's Foreign Minister following the collapse of his government) and key Allied leaders produced the Dawes Plan. Germany was allowed to make reduced reparations payments for several years, and given longer to pay overall. However, the total amount remained the same at £6,600 million.

At this time, Germany also benefited from huge loans, particularly from American investors.

In 1929 the Young Plan reduced reparations to £1,800 million and gave the German government even longer to pay it.

ACTIVITY

For both the Dawes Plan and the Young Plan complete the following information:

- Date agreed
- Reparations total (£)
- Germany given longer to pay?

THE 'GOLDEN TWENTIES'

THE POSITIVE

It seemed as if Stresemann had returned Germany to prosperity and political stability by 1928.

- Heavy industry had recovered to its pre-1914 levels.
- Exports were rising.
- Wages were increasing.
- Social welfare provision had improved.
- Infrastructure was being developed.
- There were no more *putsches*.
- The results of the 1928 **general election** indicated that people were supporting moderate rather than extremist parties.

The 1928 election resulted in the establishment of the stable Grand Coalition (so named because it involved so many of Germany's parties) under the leadership of the SPD's Hermann Müller.

Stresemann also enjoyed successes in his foreign policy.

- In 1925 he signed the Locarno Treaties by which Germany, France and Belgium agreed to accept their common borders. Shortly after French and Belgian troops withdrew from the Ruhr.
- In 1926 Germany was allowed to join the **League of Nations**. It had been refused membership of this body when it was set up in 1919, one of the results of the **Paris Peace Settlement**.
- In 1928 Germany signed up to the Kellogg–Briand Pact which stated that countries would use peaceful means to resolve disagreements.
- In 1930 the last of the Allied soldiers stationed in the Rhineland returned home.

WHAT YOU NEED TO KNOW

This period can sometimes confuse students. On the surface Germany appeared to be working well both economically and politically; however, beneath the surface the picture was very different.

THE NEGATIVE

However, much of this stability was misleading:

- Following Ebert's death in 1925, Field Marshall Paul von Hindenburg was elected President. He was not overly enthusiastic about Germany being a democracy.
- Political parties were getting on better because there was nothing important for them to fall out over. Even so, no government lasted for longer than two years.
- Industry was growing unsteadily, small businesses were under pressure from their larger rivals, agriculture was in a depression, unemployment was on the increase, welfare costs were up and the government was spending more than it was making.
- Beneath the surface there remained the desire within Germany to reverse the terms of the Treaty of Versailles.
- Germany was over-reliant on American loans. Stresemann made reference to this in early October 1929 when he spoke of Germany 'dancing on a volcano'.

ACTIVITY

Make two tables – one entitled 'Political' the other 'Economic'. Then, for each table, fill in two columns with the following headings:

- Reasons why the twenties were 'golden'
- Reasons why the twenties were not 'golden'

HITLER AND THE ORIGINS OF THE NAZI PARTY

EARLY LIFE

Adolf Hitler was born in Austria in 1889. In 1913 he went to Germany to avoid conscription. When war broke out in 1914 he joined the German army. When the conflict ended in 1918, Hitler was in hospital; he was broken-hearted when he heard about the armistice.

Following his discharge, Hitler remained in the army investigating extremist political groupings. One such group was the German Workers' Party (DAP), an extreme nationalist party set up by Anton Drexler. After attending a meeting, Hitler joined the party.

WHAT YOU NEED TO KNOW

You should know about Hitler's early life just for context. **How** he got involved with the German Workers' Party and **what** their policies were is essential knowledge.

THE NAZI PARTY

Hitler's influence over the DAP was immediate. In February 1920 it launched a new **manifesto**, the 25-Point Programme, most of which was Hitler's work. It had a range of key ideas:

- The desire to unite all Germans, with the exception of any German Jews.
- The destruction of the Treaty of Versailles.
- The need for *Lebensraum* (living space) for the German population.
- The need for strong government.

Soon after, the DAP was renamed the National Socialist German Workers' Party (NSDAP or Nazi for short). The Party also adopted the **swastika** as its symbol and bought its own newspaper, the *Völkischer Beobachter*, to help spread its ideas.

In July 1921, after threatening to resign, Hitler replaced Drexler as Party leader. In November 1921 the *Sturmabteilung* (SA) was set up as the Nazis' military wing. Members of the SA – many of whom had been in the Free Corps – were known as the Brownshirts because of their uniforms. The SA had 15,000 members a year later. Party membership also grew, but the Nazis still remained a regional party with little influence beyond Bavaria.

ACTIVITIES

1 Create a timeline of Hitler's life from 1889–1921.

2 Create a spider diagram illustrating the key points about the origins and development of the DAP/NSDAP.

THE MUNICH *PUTSCH*

PLANS

Hitler was outraged at the mess that Germany was in by late 1923. He believed that the crisis provided him with the ideal opportunity to exploit Weimar's problems and decided to stage a *putsch* in Munich followed by an attack on Berlin. On 8 November 1923, Hitler interrupted a meeting being held by the heads of the Bavarian government, police and army, Gustav von Kahr, Hans von Seisser and Otto von Lossow. He forced the leaders to announce their support for his planned rising.

FAILURE

However, once free, von Kahr, von Seisser and von Lossow organised the army to stop the intended *putsch*. On the morning of 9 November, armed police fired on a crowd of more than 2000 Nazis who were marching towards the city centre. Sixteen Nazis died in the barrage. Hitler fled and was later arrested on the charge of having committed high treason.

Hitler appeared to be finished. However, he turned his trial to his advantage, using it to condemn the government and spread his ideas. The massive media coverage of his trial provided him with more publicity than he could ever have dreamt of.

In addition, the trial judges were sympathetic to Hitler's views and at the end of the trial he was sentenced to just five years' imprisonment.

WHAT YOU NEED TO KNOW

The Munich *putsch* was the last attempt by any group to overthrow the Weimar Republic by force. You need to understand **what** Hitler was trying to do, **how** it all went wrong and **why** he got off so lightly.

ACTIVITY

Make notes about the Munich *putsch* under the following headings:

- Reasons
- Planning
- Events (draw a timeline)
- Results

NAZI REORGANISATION AND GROWTH

NEW TACTICS

Hitler only spent nine months in prison. While there he:

- wrote down his ideas in a book – *Mein Kampf* ('My Struggle')
- decided that the Nazis would gain power by standing for election, rather than by using force.

Following his release in December 1924, Hitler re-established the Nazi Party and began to set up branches across Germany, attempting to make it a national rather than regional organisation. The refounded Party was based around the Leadership Principle (*Führerprinzip*), which emphasised absolute obedience to Hitler. New Nazi groups were established including the elite *Schutzstaffel* (SS) in 1925 and the Hitler Youth, in 1926.

WHAT YOU NEED TO KNOW

It is essential that you understand **how** Hitler's experience in 1923 made him realise that he had to change tactics if he was to gain power. You should also be aware of **how** he reorganised the Nazi Party and **why** his changes had no effect in 1928.

However, the use of violence was not completely removed as a tactic. When the occasion demanded, the SA was still involved in street fights, particularly against the KPD's equivalent force, the Red Fighting League.

THE 1928 ELECTION

The reorganised Party's first electoral test came in 1928; it won only twelve seats. Since Germany appeared to be recovering both politically and economically, there seemed to be no real reason to vote for a party whose main policy was the destruction of the Weimar system.

> **ACTIVITY**
>
> Make notes about Hitler's life under these headings:
> - What Hitler did in prison
> - How long Hitler spent behind bars
> - Steps taken by Hitler after December 1924
> - New Nazi organisations set up
> - Nazi tactics
> - The 1928 election – result and reasons

GERMANY AND THE GREAT DEPRESSION

> **WHAT YOU NEED TO KNOW**
>
> The period covering the Great Depression is the most complicated part of the course. To start off, you need to understand **how** the Wall Street Crash impacted on Germany politically and economically.

ECONOMIC COLLAPSE

In October 1929 two disasters befell the Weimar Republic:

1. Gustav Stresemann died, robbing the Republic of one of its most able leaders.
2. The US economy collapsed with the **Wall Street Crash**. As a result:
   - all US investment stopped
   - those Americans who had invested in Germany insisted that their money be repaid as soon as the (mostly short term) agreements ended.

As a result, Germany's already weak economy collapsed:

- Prices and salaries fell.
- Industrial production halved.
- Businesses closed down as demand for their products dried up.
- Unemployment increased.
- Homelessness increased as people could no longer afford to meet rent payments.
- Agriculture suffered as thousands of farmers went bankrupt.

By September 1930, over 3 million Germans were unemployed (not counting part-time workers and those not registered as unemployed) while banks, unable to repay loans, were closing their doors, resulting in a loss of savings for millions.

POLITICAL COLLAPSE

Faced with these problems, the Grand Coalition began to break up and in March 1930 Chancellor Müller resigned. Heinrich Brüning of the Centre Party took over but the government remained divided. Several parties wanted to reduce welfare spending, but the SDP refused. Within months the government finally collapsed and an election was announced for September 1930. The immediate cause was the *Reichstag's* refusal to support government plans to cut spending while increasing taxation.

In this election the Nazis and Communists increased their support, with the former winning 107 seats and the latter 77. All of the parties committed to supporting Weimar and using democracy lost votes and seats in the *Reichstag*.

Brüning remained as Chancellor despite being unable to form a stable government. Unable to get parliament to agree to his laws, he was forced to ask President Hindenburg to use Article 48. For the next two years all key laws were passed in this way, fatally undermining democracy.

> **ACTIVITIES**
>
> 1. Create two spider diagrams showing the economic and political impacts of the Wall Street Crash.
> 2. Explain how Proportional Representation and Article 48 of the Weimar Constitution undermined democracy in Germany at this time. Use the following headings to help you:
>   - How proportional representation and Article 48 were meant to work
>   - How they were working in Germany in 1930

BRÜNING'S GOVERNMENT

THE 'HUNGER CHANCELLOR'

In order to avoid a repeat of the 1923 hyperinflation crisis, Brüning:

- reduced public spending
- imposed **tariffs** on imports
- slashed payments to the unemployed
- introduced salary reductions for **civil servants**.

These unpopular policies earned Brüning the nickname of 'Hunger Chancellor'. However, by late 1932 there were some signs of recovery even though unemployment stood at over 6 million. In addition, reparations were suspended in 1931 and then cancelled completely in 1932.

1932: THE YEAR OF FOUR ELECTIONS

In March and April 1932, elections were held for the post of President. Hitler received over 30 per cent of the vote. Hindenburg received just under the 50 per cent needed to win, so a second round was needed. This time, although Hitler increased his vote, Hindenburg was re-elected.

Soon after, Hindenburg forced Brüning out by telling him that he would not allow him to use Article 48 anymore. The immediate causes of his dismissal were Brüning's decisions to:

- Ban the SA and SS in April 1932 in response to high levels of violence. This concerned General Kurt von Schleicher, an influential presidential adviser. He believed that the time had come to co-operate with the Nazis.
- Divide the large landed estates in Prussia, Hindenburg's home state. This was too close to socialism for the President's liking.

VON PAPEN

On von Schleicher's advice, Hindenburg appointed Franz von Papen as Chancellor. Von Papen formed a new government, removed the ban on the SS and SA, deposed the socialist government in Prussia and called a general election for July 1932. As a result, the Nazis became the largest party with 230 seats while the KPD also increased its support.

WHAT YOU NEED TO KNOW

Brüning was Chancellor from 1930–2. His policies had an important effect on the growth of the Nazis. His successor, von Papen, also played a key part in the eventual rise of Hitler. You need to know as much as possible about the policies followed by both Chancellors.

ACTIVITIES

1. Create a spider diagram illustrating Brüning's economic policies, 1930–32.
2. Create a timeline showing the key political developments, 1930–32.
3. Write about Brüning using the following headings:
   - Party
   - Date of appointment
   - Reasons for appointment
   - Key policies
   - Date of dismissal
   - Reasons for dismissal

WHY DID SUPPORT FOR NAZISM INCREASE?

Nazi support increased for the following reasons:

- Under the direction of Joseph Goebbels, the Nazis used sophisticated **propaganda** methods. Hitler's image and ideas could be seen and heard everywhere across Germany.
- The SA grew massively in size; they attacked opponents and disrupted their meetings.
- Hitler was a talented speaker who portrayed an image of strength.
- Nazi policies focused on the groups who had been hardest hit by the depression, telling them exactly what they wanted to hear:
  - They promised jobs and the restoration of a vibrant economy to those who were starving, homeless, unemployed or had lost their businesses. The key phrase used was 'Bread and Work'.
  - They offered the overthrow of Versailles and a return to greatness to those angry at Germany's military weakness.
  - They pointed to the Jews and the Communists as groups to blame for all of Germany's problems.
- Many Germans, particularly leading industrialists such as Krupps and Thyssen, feared the growth of communism and sought the restoration of a strong government. They were, therefore, willing to support the Nazis financially. Hitler promised to destroy Germany's trade union

WHAT YOU NEED TO KNOW

Examiners will expect you to be able to identify and explain the different reasons for the Nazis' growth in popularity.

ACTIVITIES

1. Create a spider diagram summarising the different reasons for the growth in Nazi support.
2. Create a spider diagram illustrating the groups unlikely to ever vote for the Nazis.

movement when appointed Chancellor. He also enjoyed the support of Alfred Hugenberg, owner of many of the country's newspapers. He used his media empire to spread the Nazi message.

However, there were a number of groups unlikely to ever support the Nazis:

- trade unions, because the Nazis were keen to close them down
- key industrial figures, because of Nazi indiscipline
- church leaders, because they threatened Christian values
- some female voters, because of the anti-feminist nature of Nazi policies.

HITLER'S RISE TO POWER

WHAT YOU NEED TO KNOW

Between July 1932 and January 1933 there were three different Chancellors, another general election and a great deal of behind-the-door scheming. You must be clear about all of this to understand how Hitler eventually became Chancellor.

TWO ELECTIONS

Following the July 1932 election Hitler demanded the Chancellorship. Hindenburg refused and reappointed von Papen. With no support, von Papen decided to call yet another election.

The results of the November 1932 election revealed a fall in Nazi support (winning 196 seats), due to the start of economic recovery and the disappointment among some previous voters at Hitler's failure to become Chancellor. The results also showed a further increase in support for the KPD (winning 100 seats).

As leader of the largest party, Hitler again requested the position of Chancellor. Again Hindenburg refused. Von Papen wanted to stay on, planning to replace the *Reichstag* and introduce a constitution allowing a dictatorial government. He also intended to use the army to deal with any opposition. Von Schleicher told the President that this plan risked **civil war**.

INTRIGUE

Hindenburg now asked von Schleicher to take on the job himself. He lasted only 57 days, failing in his attempts to strike a deal with some Nazis and trade unionists and incurring Hindenburg's displeasure for requesting the use of Article 48.

Meanwhile others were trying to persuade the President to appoint Hitler. Particularly involved in this was von Papen, who assured Hindenburg that he would be able to control the Nazi leader. Hindenburg was also being advised by his son, Oskar, to appoint Hitler. At the same time key business leaders and landowners were asking Hindenburg to create a stable and effective government. On 30 January 1933, therefore, Hindenburg finally appointed Hitler as chancellor.

ACTIVITIES

1. Create a timeline showing the key political developments, 1932–33.
2. Write about Papen and Schleicher using the following headings:
   - Party
   - Date of appointment
   - Reasons for appointment
   - Key policies
   - Date of dismissal
   - Reasons for dismissal

NAZI GERMANY, 1933–9

NAZI CONSOLIDATION OF POWER (I)

WHAT YOU NEED TO KNOW

You need to be able to identify the obstacles to Hitler's achievement of dictatorship and **what** he did in 1933 to overcome them.

THE *REICHSTAG* FIRE

To achieve dictatorship Hitler still had to deal with the President, the *Reichstag* and the army. In addition there might be opposition from other parties, Germany's state governments or trade unions.

To gain an overall majority in the *Reichstag*, Hitler called fresh elections for 5 March 1933. If he wanted to achieve a majority, he had to stop people voting for the SPD and KPD. Therefore:

- In early February a new law forbade newspapers and public meetings from criticising Hitler and his government.
- In the state of Prussia – which made up 66 per cent of Germany – leading Nazi Hermann Göring was Minister of the Interior. He enrolled the SA into the police and used them to disrupt other parties' election campaigns.
- The burning of the *Reichstag* building on 27 February was blamed on the Communists as Marinus van der Lubbe – a Dutch Communist – was captured at the scene. Although many remained suspicious that

the Nazis were involved in setting the fire, it gave Hitler the chance to damage the KPD's campaign and to persuade Hindenburg to approve the decree *For the Protection of the People and State*. This law gave the government the power to suspend many of Weimar's civil rights. The government proceeded to **intern** opponents, disrupt other parties' election campaigns and intimidate left-wing voters.

The Nazis won 288 seats in the election – still not an overall majority. The KPD won 81 seats while the SPD won 120. With the support of the 52 Nationalist Party Deputies, the Nazis could now count on just over 50 per cent of *Reichstag* votes.

ENABLING ACT

Hitler then moved to amend the constitution to allow the government to introduce laws without the *Reichstag*'s approval for a period of four years. Such a change required the support of two-thirds of the *Reichstag* members present.

To achieve this majority Hitler simply ensured that most opponents were not there to vote against the measure. He used the decree *For the Protection of the People and State* to ban the KPD. With the KPD unable to vote, Hitler just needed the support of the Catholic Centre Party to achieve the 66 per cent of votes needed. This was achieved by a promise to cancel the decree *For the Protection of the People and State* and an agreement to protect the rights of the Catholic Church. When it came to the vote, it was passed by 441 votes to 94. Only the Social Democrats opposed the measure.

Gleichschaltung

Within months Hitler had eliminated most of the remaining political opposition in Germany as the government implemented *Gleichschaltung* (co-ordination of all aspects of life to fit in with Nazi ideals):

- In late March all state parliaments were closed down and then re-established with Nazi majorities.
- In April 1933, Jews and other political enemies were removed from jobs in the legal profession and civil service. At the same time key positions within Germany's state governments were taken over by Nazis.
- In May all trade unions were outlawed and replaced by a Nazi union, the DAF (German Labour Front).
- In July Germany became a one-party state. However, by this stage the Social Democrats had already been outlawed, while the Centre Party had dissolved itself.
- In December 1933 new *Reichstag* elections were held. This time the Nazis won 92 per cent of the vote.
- In January 1934 Hitler introduced the *Law for the Reconstruction of the State*. This abolished all of Germany's state governments apart from Prussia's, which was to be run by Herman Göring.

ACTIVITIES

1. Create a timeline showing the key political developments, 1933–34.
2. Make notes about the *Reichstag* fire under the following headings:
   - Date
   - How Hitler used the fire to his advantage
   - What the decree *For the Protection of the People and State* allowed the Nazis to do
3. Make a table with three columns about the Enabling Act, using the following headings:
   - Why Hitler wanted it
   - How it was passed
   - What it meant

NAZI CONSOLIDATION OF POWER (II)

WHAT YOU NEED TO KNOW

The year 1934 marks the move towards the final achievement of dictatorship. You need to understand **why** Hitler had to move against his own movement, **how** he did this and **how** his actions gained him the support of the army.

DIVISIONS WITHIN

Hitler's position was still under threat; however, now the danger came from the 2-million strong SA, commanded for the last two years by Ernst Röhm.

Röhm was one of the more left-wing members of the Nazi Party. He believed that Hitler's take-over would be followed by a second revolution in which the power of Germany's economic old guard and the army would be crushed and the SA would become Germany's new army. Röhm now wanted this second revolution to start.

Röhm's plans worried the army. This concerned Hitler as:

- The army could still stop his achievement of dictatorship.
- He needed the army to implement his foreign policy.

Röhm was also opposed by other leading Nazis such as Heinrich Himmler and Göring. They believed that he had become too big for his boots and tried to convince Hitler that Röhm was disloyal and that aspects of his private life – Röhm was a homosexual – were inappropriate for a leading Nazi.

THE NIGHT OF THE LONG KNIVES

Hitler finally acted on the night of 30 June 1934, an event that became known as the 'Night of the Long Knives'. Anyone suspected of preventing his achievement of dictatorship was executed. Key SA leaders, including Röhm, were eliminated. So too were a number of earlier rivals such as Gustav von Kahr and General von Schleicher.

It is believed around 100 people were killed. The Nazis justified their actions by claiming that they had prevented an SA *putsch*. On 3 July the *Reichstag* passed a law making the actions taken on the Night of the Long Knives legal.

FÜHRER

Hindenburg was now the only person standing in the way of Hitler's dictatorship, but he died on 2 August 1934. A day earlier a new law had been passed which merged together the jobs of President and Chancellor and replaced them with the all-powerful position of *Führer* and *Reich* Chancellor.

The army now demonstrated their gratitude for the eradication of the SA threat by swearing an oath of personal loyalty to the *Führer*. Previously soldiers had promised their loyalty to the constitution.

Shortly after, the German people were asked to vote in a plebiscite to indicate their approval for Hitler's new position. Almost 90 per cent (43 million) of those who voted agreed with the actions taken.

ACTIVITIES

1 Create a timeline showing the key political developments in 1934.

2 Explain the reasons, events and impact of the Night of the Long Knives.

3 The following were sources of weakness for Hitler. How did he overcome each?

- SA
- Hindenburg
- Army

4 Match the solution to the weakness to show how each was overcome. Remember that one solution might have helped to overcome more than one weakness.

Weakness	Solution
Reichstag	Night of the Long Knives
Cabinet	Army Oath of Loyalty
Hindenburg	Law for the Protection of the People and State
Army	Enabling Act
Trade unions	1933 election
State governments	
Other parties	
SA	

NAZI ECONOMIC POLICY (I): UNIONS AND UNEMPLOYMENT

WHAT YOU NEED TO KNOW

This is a crucial area for you to get to grips with. Economic collapse had helped Hitler gain power and people expected a lot from him in this area. You need to know **what** he did to reduce the power of the unions and tackle the huge levels of unemployment.

DESTROYING THE UNIONS

Hitler was afraid that trade unions could interfere with his plans and so in May 1933 they were outlawed and strikes were declared illegal. Unions were replaced by the German Labour Front (DAF – *Deutsche Arbeitsfront*) led by Dr Robert Ley. Within two years all workers – over 20 million people – were members. A branch of the DAF, the Beauty of Labour (SdA – *Schönheit der Arbeit*) was set up to improve working conditions.

The DAF was meant to represent the workers in discussions with the employers. However, in reality it tended to side with employers and workers found their freedoms restricted (for example, their ability to move jobs) and their working hours increased. On a positive note, wages improved a little and prices and rents were strictly controlled by the state.

FREE TIME

The Nazis also wanted workers to be happy outside the workplace. Therefore Strength Through Joy (KDF – *Kraft Durch Freude*) was established in November 1933 to improve workers' free time. The KDF, also led by Ley, provided cheap holidays and organised a broad range of sporting activities. Workers were also given the chance to pay into a savings scheme to own a car, the *Volkswagen* (people's car). However, no cars had been distributed when the war started in 1939.

UNEMPLOYMENT

The Nazis' vote had increased partly as a result of their promises to get Germans back to work. At first glance it would seem that they were

ACTIVITY

1 Make notes under the following headings about the destruction of the trade unions:

- Why it was done
- How it was done
- What it meant for workers
- What it meant for the state

largely successful, with only 300,000 Germans listed as unemployed by 1939. This was achieved in a number of ways:

1 The scale of existing public work schemes was increased with the establishment of the National Labour Service (RAD – *Reichsarbeitsdienst*). The RAD – which brought together similar schemes begun by earlier governments – built schools, hospitals and motorways. Six-month membership became compulsory for all men aged 18–25 in 1935.
2 Many people – especially professional women and Jews – were forced from the workplace and their jobs then given to the unemployed. Neither of these groups was then counted as unemployed.
3 The introduction of conscription in 1935 helped reduce unemployment levels. In 1933 there were 100,000 in the army. By 1939 there were 1.4 million.
4 As Germany prepared for war, thousands of jobs were created in the armament and associated industries (for example, steel and coal). Likewise, the drive for **autarky** led to the creation of new industries focused on creating synthetic replacements for raw materials.

ACTIVITIES

2 Write information for the DAF and KDF, including:
- Purpose
- Leader
- Tactics
- Reasons it was good for workers
- Reasons it was bad for workers

3 Create a spider diagram showing the strategies that were introduced to reduce unemployment.

NAZI ECONOMIC POLICY (II): STABILITY AND AUTARKY

WHAT YOU NEED TO KNOW

Economic recovery was also essential for Hitler's foreign policy objectives. You need to know **what** he did to achieve his objectives and be able to assess **how successful** he was.

NEW PLAN

In May 1933 respected economist Dr Hjalmar Schacht became President of the *Reichsbank*. Within a year he became Minister of Economics. Schacht's 1934 New Plan – introduced to deal with a **trade deficit** – oversaw the revitalisation of the economy by:

- introducing massive cuts to welfare spending
- imposing limits on imports
- implementing a series of trade agreements with countries that ensured that Germany was supplied with vital raw materials in return for goods manufactured in Germany
- introducing targeted government spending on key industries.

The German economy recovered within two years; however, this was not enough to ensure Schacht's survival. By 1936 Hitler was pressurising him to increase spending on military resources. Schacht was unwilling to do this as he feared that it would damage the recovery. As a result he was increasingly ignored by Hitler and a year later he resigned.

FOUR-YEAR PLAN

Despite his total lack of economic expertise, Hermann Göring was appointed to create an economy that was ready for war (*Wehrwirtschaft*). In 1936 he introduced the Four-Year Plan. Its aim was to ensure that Germany had become an autarky in advance of any future conflict through:

- constructing new factories
- placing industries under strict government control
- cutting the amount of goods imported
- setting higher targets for the production of materials such as oil, rubber and steel
- encouraging industries to develop *ersatz* – synthetic substitutes for raw materials, particularly rubber and oil
- imposing targets for the production of foodstuffs. The *Reich* Food Estate, which all farmers had to join, provided strict rules on what and how much should be produced.

However, by 1939 Germany was still importing over one-third of the natural resources it needed. It had become clear that the only way to make its economy self-sufficient would be to conquer other countries to gain access to their natural resources.

ACTIVITY

Make notes about the New Plan and the Four-Year Plan under the following headings:
- Purpose
- Person in charge
- Strategies introduced
- Areas of success
- Areas of failure

HITLER IN CONTROL

To ensure the loyalty of all Germans to the state and Führer, the Nazis sought the creation of a *Volksgemeinschaft* (people's community).

To support the Führer a control system was established across the country:

- *Reichsleiter* – leading Nazis
- *Gauleiter* – provincial leaders
- *Kreisleiter* – regional leaders
- *Ortsgruppeführer* – local group leaders
- *Zellenleiters* – cell leaders
- *Blockleiter* – local leaders.

While this system helped ensure that the party was aware of the mood, thoughts and behaviour of the population, establishing total control required even greater interference. There was no group or institution within Germany that the Nazi government did not try to control.

WHAT YOU NEED TO KNOW

You need to understand three things about Nazi control policies:

1. **Why** they wanted to control each aspect.
2. **What** steps they took to ensure control.
3. **How** successful each of these policies was.

ACTIVITY

Create a flow diagram illustrating how the Nazis' system of control operated.

WOMEN

For the Nazis, women's role was summed up by the Three Ks – *Kinder, Kirche und Küche* (Children, Church and Cooking). A number of strategies were implemented to achieve this:

- Women were encouraged to dress in a traditional German manner and not to wear make-up.
- Some women – particularly those married or in the professions (such as medicine or law) – were forced from the workplace.
- Every newly-married couple was given a loan of 1,000 marks and 25 per cent of this was written off for every child born. The *Law for the Encouragement of Marriage* of June 1933 encouraged women to marry and have large families.
- An award called the Motherhood Cross was created to encourage women to have as many children as possible. These women were also able to benefit from lower taxation and increased benefits.
- Contraception and abortion became much harder to obtain.
- Dieting and smoking were discouraged in case they interfered with pregnancy and childbirth.
- Divorce to end childless marriages was made easier to obtain.
- Unmarried mothers were encouraged to live in homes (*Lebensborn* – Spring of Life) where **Aryan** SS men could impregnate them.

At the same time, the Nazis were looking for the birth rate to improve only if it resulted in a greater number of healthy Aryan offspring. The 1935 Marriage Law demanded evidence of racial purity and health before marriages could go ahead. Women deemed to be unfit mothers or likely to produce unhealthy children faced sterilisation. By 1939 an estimated 350,000 women had been dealt with in this way.

These policies had mixed results:

- The birth rate had increased by 1939, but remained lower than during the 'Golden Twenties'.
- The numbers getting married increased at first, but was levelling off by 1935.
- Many women kept their jobs because of a lack of replacement workers although the numbers of professional women did go down.
- The number of women in jobs actually rose in the later 1930s as the drive for rearmament and autarky took off.

WHAT YOU NEED TO KNOW

You need to explain **what** role the Nazis saw women having in Germany, **how** they went about achieving their aim and **how** successful they were.

ACTIVITIES

1. Create a spider diagram showing the different strategies the Nazis used towards women.
2. Give evidence for and against whether the Nazis' birth rate and female employment policies worked.
3. Analyse the success of Nazi policies towards women using the headings of (i) Successes and (ii) Failures.

YOUTH

INSIDE SCHOOL

The Nazis saw **indoctrination** of the youth with their ideas as the key to their future control of Germany. To this end they set about influencing children inside and outside school.

Inside school the Nazis sought to train students to accept that 'individuals must be willing and ready to sacrifice themselves for Nation and *Führer*'. Therefore they:

- dismissed Jewish teachers and those regarded as unreliable
- encouraged teachers to join the NSLB (National Socialist Teachers' League). Within six years all but three per cent had joined up.
- Nazified the curriculum to reflect the importance of subjects such as history, biology, geography and PE (which was allowed to take up 15 per cent of the timetable)
- prepared boys for life in the military and girls for their role as mothers
- established special schools (*Napolas* and Adolf Hitler Schools) to teach Germany's future leaders. High flying boys went to *Ordensburgen* (Castles of Order).

WHAT YOU NEED TO KNOW

Be clear about **why** young people were so important to the Nazis and make sure you can explain **what** they did to ensure control.

FREE TIME

The Hitler Youth Movement controlled the activities of young people outside the classroom. Led by Baldur von Schirach, membership became compulsory for certain ages in 1936 and for most others in 1939. By that stage there were more than 7 million members.

The table below shows the different sections to the movement.

Age	Boys' Organisation	Girls' Organisation
6–10	Pimpfen (Cubs)	
10–14	*Deutsches Jungvolk* (Young German Folk)	*Jung Mädel* (Young Girls)
14–18	*Hitler Jugend* (Hitler Youth)	*Bund Deutscher Mädel* (League of German Girls)
18–21		*Glaube und Schönheit* (Faith and Beauty)

The Nazis' youth policies had mixed results. Most young people did not oppose them and would have been influenced by the Nazi policies both inside and outside the classroom. However, the quality and breadth of education suffered badly, with traditional subjects losing out.

A significant minority (perhaps as many as 1 million) avoided joining the Nazi youth movements. Some of these even established rival youth groups. The two most notable were the Edelweiss Pirates and the Swing Youth.

ACTIVITIES

1. Create a spider diagram illustrating the strategies the Nazis used inside schools to ensure control.
2. Create a spider diagram explaining the different parts of the Hitler Youth Movement.
3. Analyse the success of Nazi youth policies using the headings of (i) Successes and (ii) Failures.

RELIGION

Hitler knew that it would be almost impossible to destroy Germany's religions; however, he was determined to limit their influence as much as possible.

WHAT YOU NEED TO KNOW

Control of religions was essential as their beliefs represented a threat to the regime. You need to know **how** the state dealt with the different Churches and understand what its own religion was all about.

CATHOLICISM

In July 1933 a **concordat** was signed with the Catholic Church. The Church agreed not to involve itself in politics and in return it was permitted to continue to run its own schools and youth activities. By 1936 some of the terms – particularly those relating to youth groups – were being ignored. In 1937 Pope Pius XI responded by condemning the Nazi regime and later some German Church leaders, such as Bishop Clemens von Galen of Münster, spoke out strongly and successfully against Nazi policies such as euthanasia of the mentally ill.

LUTHERANISM

The **Lutheran** Church was divided in its attitude to **Nazism**. Pro-Nazi Lutherans were known as German Christians. Their symbol was a cross with the swastika at its centre while their version of the Bible was altered to ensure many references to the Jews were omitted. They were led by Ludwig Müller who became the first Reich Bishop in July 1933. In 1934 those Lutherans who disagreed with Nazism set up the Confessional Church. One of their leaders was Pastor Martin Niemöller who was arrested by the Nazis in 1937 and sent to Dachau **concentration camp**.

THE NAZI CHURCH

The Nazis created their own Church, the German Faith Movement. Its beliefs owed much more to pagan values (such as sun worship) than to the ideas of Christianity and attracted few members.

Overall the Nazis were unsuccessful in their aim of undermining the power of Germany's Churches; however they were able to reduce their influence. Although a number of individual clerics spoke out against aspects of the regime, by and large the Churches remained more concerned about ensuring their survival.

ACTIVITY

Make a table to show the areas of success and the areas of failure for the Nazis' policies towards the following Churches:

- Catholics
- Lutherans
- German Faith Movement

THE POLICE STATE

WHAT YOU NEED TO KNOW

You need to be able to explain:

1. **What** the police state was.
2. **How** it worked.
3. **Whether or not** it was successful.

'PROTECTIVE CUSTODY'

The decree *For the Protection of the People and State* allowed for opponents to be arrested and placed in 'protective custody' in concentration camps, the first of which was established at Dachau in March 1933. By mid-1934 these camps were being run by the SS's Death's Head Units.

While most early inmates tended to be political prisoners, before long other groups suffered internment including:

- criminals
- gypsies
- tramps
- the 'work shy'
- the 'anti-social'
- homosexuals
- Jews.

All of these prisoners had to endure extremely harsh conditions in the concentration camps.

SECURITY FORCES

Following the Night of the Long Knives, Himmler's SS took over responsibility for party security from the SA. Along with the Gestapo (see below) and SD (both branches of the SS), the SS removed any real or potential opponents of the state. Historians argue that the SS became so powerful that it became a 'state within a state'.

The Gestapo (*GEheime STAats POlizei* – the secret state police), also led by Himmler, arrested opponents (known as 'enemies of the state'). Much of the information it worked on came from ordinary Germans denouncing their fellow countrymen. The SD (*Sicherheitdienst*) was the intelligence arm of the SS; headed by Himmler's protégé Reinhard Heydrich, it monitored the security of the *Reich*.

ACTIVITIES

1. Create a spider diagram showing the different groups that ended up in concentration camps.
2. Make notes on the SS, Gestapo and SD under the following headings:
   - Group
   - Leader
   - Function
3. Analyse the Nazi police state using the headings of (i) Successes and (ii) Failures.

JUDICIARY

The judicial system came under state control. The aim was to ensure that the legal system did not protect those that the state wanted to punish. Special People's Courts were established in 1934 to judge those accused of crimes against the state. It is estimated that up to 1939 the judicial system sentenced nearly a quarter of a million Germans found guilty of political crimes to more than 600,000 years in prison.

Overall, the police state was very successful. Although individuals might have grumbled about aspects of the Nazi state, in general there was no organised opposition until the Second World War.

PROPAGANDA

Getting people to support the new government was the job of Dr Joseph Göbbels, Minister for Popular Enlightenment and Propaganda. To help him in this task, Göbbels established the Reich Chamber of Culture. This was subdivided into six sections, one for each major propaganda method.

One of the most impressive propaganda methods the Nazis used were the annual Nuremberg rallies, attended by as many as 500,000 people. Light, sound and costume were used to create a mesmeric atmosphere. Other smaller-scale rallies were held in other parts of Germany throughout the year. The high point of Nazi propaganda efforts probably came with the spectacle of the 1936 Berlin Olympics.

WHAT YOU NEED TO KNOW

Propaganda was one of the key Nazi methods of control. You should be able to identify the different methods the Nazis used and explain whether or not they worked.

CONTROLLING THE MEDIA

Control of the media was also a key aim. This was achieved in a variety of ways:

- Most newspapers were bought up by *Eher Verlag*, the Nazi publishers. By 1939 the Nazis owned 69 per cent of the newspaper titles in circulation.
- The *Editors' Law* held editors responsible for the content of their newspapers.
- Only journalists that were approved by the government could work in the media.
- Newspapers that printed stories the regime disapproved of were shut down.
- Editors went to a daily Propaganda Ministry briefing to be told what to print.
- The Nazis took control of all radio stations.
- People were encouraged to buy cheap radios made by the *Reich* Radio Company. These 'People's Receivers' could only pick up Nazi broadcasts. By 1939, 70 per cent of households owned one, the highest percentage of radio ownership for any country in the world.
- Loudspeakers were erected in public places and in workplaces.

The Propaganda Ministry also controlled **censorship**. It censored cinema, theatre, music and literature. In the case of the latter, 20,000 books were symbolically burned in Berlin in May 1933.

The 1934 law against malicious gossip outlawed anti-Nazi stories and jokes.

Exhibitions of 'degenerate' art were organised showing people the 'distorted' work of modern artists such as George Grosz and Otto Dix. Such art was unfavourably compared with the realism of Nazi art. Unacceptable music such as jazz was condemned. The writings of over 2,500 authors were banned. Propaganda films such as *The Eternal Jew* were produced to portray the Jewish race in an unflattering way. Listening to foreign radio broadcasts was also made illegal.

Nazi propaganda probably helped reinforce existing beliefs but was less successful in getting people to accept new ideas. Censorship ensured that the quality of much of Germany's culture was damaged. Only in the area of cinema was high-quality work produced, particularly by Leni Riefenstahl.

ACTIVITIES

1 Complete the following table:

Area to control	Methods used
Newspapers	
Radio	

2 Create a spider diagram illustrating all of the different propaganda and censorship methods used by the Nazis.

3 Analyse Nazi propaganda using the headings of (i) Successes and (ii) Failures.

ANTI-SEMITISM AND THE PERSECUTION OF MINORITIES

Within Germany there was a belief that the country's relatively small number of Jews were more influential than they should have been. Hitler and the Nazis used propaganda to tell Germans that Jews were to blame for many of Germany's problems.

Allied to this were the Nazis' master race theories – the belief in the existence of a *Herrenvolk* or Aryan race, a master race of human beings who were superior to and who would eventually overcome all other races (the *Untermenschen*), including the Jews.

It wasn't only the Jews, however, that the Nazis saw as *Untermenschen*. They also viewed groups such as those listed on page 16, as well as the mentally and physically disabled, prostitutes, alcoholics, **Jehovah's Witnesses**,

WHAT YOU NEED TO KNOW

Nazi policy towards the Jews and other groups deemed to be undesirable is one of the key elements of the GCSE course. You must be able to explain the different stages of the policy. Remember that your course does not require you to write about the Final Solution/ Holocaust.

and other minority groups as lesser beings. They enacted policies designed to prevent them from reproducing, to remove them from society or to eliminate them altogether.

However, the Nazis reserved their greatest hatred for Germany's Jews and so once in power, Hitler wasted no time in putting his **anti-Semitism** into operation:

April 1933	**Boycott** of Jewish shops introduced. Jews banned from government jobs.
September 1933	Jews banned from owning land.
October 1933	Jews banned from key media jobs.
September 1935	Nuremberg Laws. There were two main elements: • Jews were deprived of many political and economic rights (*Reich* Citizenship Law). • It was illegal for Jews and Aryans to marry or engage in sexual relations outside marriage (Law for the Protection of German Blood and German Honour).
May 1935	Jews banned from joining the army.
August 1936	Persecution of the Jews eased off during the 1936 Olympic Games, which were held in Berlin.
January 1937	Jews banned from the key professions including teaching, accountancy and dentistry.
April 1938	Jews ordered to register all wealth and property.
June 1938	Jews to register all businesses.
July/August 1938	Jews had to carry identity cards.
September 1938	Jews banned from all legal practices.
October 1938	Jews to have their passports stamped with a J-shaped symbol. Jews forced to use new names: Israel for men, Sarah for women.
November 1938	The murder of a Nazi diplomat by a Jew in Paris on 7 November led to a massive outbreak of anti-Jewish persecution known as *Kristallnacht*. More than 400 synagogues and 7,500 shops were destroyed. Ninety-one Jews were killed and over the following months 20,000 were sent to concentration camps. The Nazis fined the Jews 1 billion marks for the damage caused on *Kristallnacht*. They also had to clean up the streets in the aftermath of the attacks.
November 1938	Remaining Jewish businesses confiscated or closed down.
November 1938	Jews not allowed to attend German schools.
January 1939	Jews encouraged to emigrate from Germany.
January 1939	Hitler spoke of future annihilation of Jews.
July 1939	Jews forbidden from holding government jobs.

A combination of support (especially resulting from propaganda), education, ignorance or fear ensured that persecution of the Jews was able to go ahead.

ACTIVITIES

1. Create a spider diagram illustrating the key elements of the Nazis' policies towards the Jews.
2. Explain the reasons for, events and results of *Kristallnacht*.

NAZI POLICIES AND ACTIONS IN EUROPE, 1933–41

NAZI FOREIGN POLICY

AIMS

Hitler had three main foreign policy aims:

1. To restore the strength of Germany's armed forces by removing the restrictions imposed by the Treaty of Versailles.
2. To unite all those claiming German nationality into the Third Reich (*Grossdeutschland*).
3. To create *Lebensraum* (living space) by acquiring new territory from racially inferior Central and Eastern Europe states (especially the USSR) to support the needs of the growing German population.

At first, Hitler moved cautiously in his foreign policy, but within a few years, as his dictatorship strengthened and as Germany's military strength began to return, he moved rapidly to achieve his aims.

DISARMAMENT

At the 1919 **Paris Peace Conference** it had been agreed that all countries would disarm. However, Germany was the only country that did so. It was then decided that an international conference would be held in Geneva to resolve this problem. It first met in 1932.

At the conference Germany demanded that the other major powers disarm. The French government refused and in response Germany walked out of the conference and withdrew from the League of Nations. At the same time Hitler signed a Non-Aggression Pact with Poland in January 1934.

REARMAMENT

Throughout the 1920s, Germany used its friendship with the USSR to help rebuild its military strength, despite the restrictions imposed by the Treaty of Versailles. At first, Hitler continued with this cautious policy, but once he felt secure in power, military expenditure tripled to 9 billion marks and rearmament speeded up:

- The navy began to construct new vessels, including submarines.
- The air force (***Luftwaffe***) was officially set up in 1935; it soon had over 2,500 aircraft.
- Conscription was publicly announced in March 1935 although the army had already quadrupled in size from the official 100,000 set at Versailles.

All of these actions broke the terms of the Treaty Versailles. In response the leaders of Britain, Italy and France met in Stresa in April 1935 to condemn Germany's actions. However, within weeks this partnership had collapsed. This was because Germany and Britain signed a naval agreement in June 1935, which permitted Germany to increase its fleet until it was 35 per cent of the size of the Royal Navy.

This agreement was a massive diplomatic victory for Hitler:

- The anti-German (Stresa) coalition was broken up.
- The German navy could now increase massively.
- One of the countries that had created the Treaty of Versailles was involved in the breaking of its terms.

There were also other successes for Hitler at this time. The Versailles settlement had provided for a future plebiscite to decide who would control the Saar region. This vote finally took place in January 1935. Nearly 91 per cent voted for a return to German rule.

WHAT YOU NEED TO KNOW

You need to know **what** Hitler wanted to achieve with his foreign policy. You should be clear about his initial policies in the years 1933–35, and **how** Britain and France responded to them.

ACTIVITIES

1. Create a spider diagram illustrating Hitler's main foreign policy objectives.
2. Create a timeline of developments in foreign policy 1933–35.
3. Make notes under the following headings concerning rearmament:
   - Developments pre-Hitler
   - Why Germany withdrew from the 1932 Disarmament Conference
   - Rearmament under Hitler 1933–35
   - Steps taken to speed up rearmament
   - Allied reaction (Stresa Front)
4. Analyse the 1935 Anglo–German Naval Agreement using the following headings:
   - Reasons
   - Details
   - Impact

A KEY YEAR – 1936

THE RHINELAND

Hitler detested the fact that the Treaty of Versailles had left Germany's border with France undefended. Therefore, in March 1936, thousands of German troops and policemen reoccupied the hitherto demilitarised Rhineland, an act that violated the terms of both the Versailles and Locarno Treaties. Hitler was testing the waters to see how the Allies would react. He knew that German forces were still comparatively weak and had even ordered them to retreat if challenged.

However, France and Britain took no action, preferring to achieve a peaceful solution. This strategy became known as **appeasement** and allowed Germany to expand with no action being taken to stop them until 1939. Neville Chamberlain (British Prime Minister 1937–40) strongly supported appeasement. This policy increased Hitler's belief in the Allies' weakness.

Hitler's success in the Rhineland gave a massive boost to his popularity at home. In a plebiscite held in late March to allow Germans to give their opinions on the remilitarisation, all but one per cent of those that voted supported Hitler's actions.

ALLIANCES

Hitler also moved to ensure that Germany would not be alone if a war was ever to break out. By the end of 1936 military agreements had been made with:

- Italy (the Rome–Berlin Axis)
- Japan (the Anti-Comintern Pact).

Hitler also got involved in the Spanish Civil War (1936–9). He sent the *Luftwaffe*, flying as the Condor Legion, to perfect bombing techniques. He hoped to:

- help establish a like-minded system
- secure another ally.

By 1936 it was clear that Hitler was intending to go to war. In that year he gave Göring the task of overseeing the creation of a war economy through the Four-Year Plan. A year later, as recorded in the **Hossbach Memorandum**, Hitler secretly told his generals that he could see Germany being involved in a major war by the mid-1940s.

WHAT YOU NEED TO KNOW

The year 1936 is key in Hitler's foreign policy as he began to flex his military muscles for the first time. Make sure you are aware about **what** he did and **how** it impacted on international relations. In particular, be clear about what appeasement was.

ACTIVITIES

1. Create a timeline of developments in German foreign policy in 1936–37.
2. Analyse the remilitarisation of the Rhineland using the following headings:
   - Reasons
   - Events
   - Result
3. Write a sentence to explain each of the following foreign policy developments 1936–37:
   - Rome–Berlin Axis
   - Anti-Comintern Pact
   - Spanish Civil War
   - Four-Year Plan
   - Hossbach Memorandum

ANSCHLUSS

FAILURE

In July 1934, Nazis in Austria attempted to seize power. However, Hitler failed to support them because:

- Germany was still militarily weak
- Italy had threatened to intervene militarily to stop Austria from becoming a Nazi-controlled state.

By 1938, things were very different:

- Italy was now Germany's closest ally.
- Secret contacts with France and Britain indicated that they would not oppose Germany gaining control of Austria.
- Austria was economically weak and more likely to be open to increased links with an increasingly prosperous Germany.
- Hitler felt that Germany was strong enough militarily to attempt an *Anschluss*.

WHAT YOU NEED TO KNOW

Do you know **why** Hitler wanted an *Anschluss*, **how** he went about achieving it and **what** the Allies did in response? These are key elements in any analysis of Nazi foreign policy in 1938.

SUCCESS

In early 1938 Hitler forced Austrian Chancellor Schuschnigg into appointing Nazis to his government. Schuschnigg was so concerned about the impact of Hitler's increased influence that he announced there would be a plebiscite over Austria's future. He hoped that Austrians would use the opportunity to vote against an *Anschluss*.

Hitler was outraged and demanded that Schuschnigg cancel the plebiscite and resign as Chancellor. Schuschnigg agreed and was replaced by Artur Seyss-Inquart, an Austrian National Socialist. Seyss-Inquart then asked Hitler to send his army into Austria. With no one to oppose them, the troops began to move in on 12 March 1938. On the next day Hitler announced that the *Anschluss* had taken place and Austria had become part of Germany. A subsequent referendum on the *Anschluss* resulted in 99 per cent approval for the action.

Versailles had again been broken and, by acquiring territory not held before, Hitler was now moving forward with his plans for a *Grossdeutschland*. In addition, Germany had gained access to the resources of the Austrian Army. Again the Allies protested but did nothing else, thus encouraging further expansion.

ACTIVITY

Analyse the *Anschluss* using the following headings:

- Reasons
- Events
- Results

CZECHOSLOVAKIA

WHAT YOU NEED TO KNOW

Czechoslovakia is probably the most complicated part of Hitler's foreign policy. Try to understand exactly **what** happened, **why** it happened and **what** the implications for European peace were. Again, be aware that appeasement plays a key part here.

THE SUDETEN CRISIS

Hitler's next target was Czechoslovakia. It had a sizeable German minority. Hitler:

- launched a misinformation campaign against the Czech government, arguing that it was allowing the mistreatment of the 3 million Germans living in the industrially-developed Sudetenland region
- encouraged the pro-Nazi Sudeten German Party, led by Konrad Henlein, to make impossible demands of the Czech government and to engage in civil unrest when these demands were not granted.

British Prime Minister Neville Chamberlain was so concerned about the prospect of war that he flew to meet Hitler in September 1938. At this meeting Hitler demanded that Germany be given all parts of the Sudetenland that were over 50 per cent German. Britain and France persuaded Czechoslovakia to accept these demands.

Hitler now upped the pressure by demanding that all of the Sudetenland be handed over to him by 1 October. This time the Czechs refused and negotiations broke down. With war seemingly inevitable, another meeting was organised for Munich. Before this meeting took place, Hitler declared that once he had gained the Sudetenland he would demand territory off no other European country.

MUNICH

Apart from Chamberlain and Hitler, the conference was attended by the leaders of France (Édouard Daladier) and Italy (Benito Mussolini). Amazingly, however, Czechoslovakia's leader, Edvard Beneš, was excluded and Czechoslovakia's ally, the Soviet Union, was not invited.

There were three main terms in the agreement reached:

1. Germany would gain the Sudetenland.
2. Hitler agreed to the holding of plebiscites in mixed areas of Czechoslovakia (to work out the wishes of the other minority groups in the country).
3. Germany promised to respect the independence of the rest of Czechoslovakia.

ACTIVITIES

1. Create a timeline illustrating the key developments with regard to Czechoslovakia **before** the Munich Conference.
2. Analyse the Munich Conference using the following headings:
   - Why it took place
   - Who was there
   - Who was not there
   - What was decided
   - What did Germany promise

THE ROAD TO WAR

BROKEN PROMISES

In March 1939, Hitler forced the Czech government to hand over the provinces of Bohemia and Moravia (which had German minorities). For the first time Hitler had taken over non-German territory. Days later the remaining parts of Czechoslovakia were also dealt with. Slovakia came under German protection while the province of Ruthenia was handed over to Hungary, which had supported Germany's foreign policy.

Britain and France issued yet another protest. Not surprisingly Hitler paid no heed to their condemnations and continued in the same vein by successfully demanding the former German port of Memel from Lithuania, which had seized the port in 1923.

NAZI–SOVIET PACT

In March 1939 Hitler turned his attention to Poland. His initial demands were for the return of Danzig and the provision of a road and rail link across the Polish corridor to connect East Prussia with the rest of Germany.

Britain and France offered Poland a security guarantee on 30 March 1939. Hitler chose to ignore their actions. Germany stated it no longer supported the 1934 Non-Aggression Pact and preparations for an invasion were stepped up. Perhaps to guarantee that he had an ally, a full military alliance, the Pact of Steel, was signed with Italy in May.

Tied in with *Lebensraum* was Hitler's desire for the destruction of Communist Russia allied with access to its immense natural resources, including oil. Other powers were amazed, therefore, when on 23 August 1939, Nazi Germany and Soviet Russia, two countries whose political ideas were completely opposed, signed the Nazi–Soviet Pact.

As well as agreeing not to attack each other for ten years, the Pact contained a secret agreement to divide Poland up between both countries. This left Germany free to attack Poland without taking the risk of having to face opposition from Russian troops.

As far as Hitler was concerned, the Nazi–Soviet Pact cancelled out any threat of Britain and France defending Poland. On 1 September 1939, therefore, Germany launched an invasion of Poland. Two days later Britain and France responded by declaring war upon Germany.

WHAT YOU NEED TO KNOW

This section looks at the final countdown to war. The highlight is the Nazi–Soviet Pact so make sure you understand what it was all about.

ACTIVITIES

1. Create a timeline showing the key developments in foreign policy during 1939.
2. Analyse the Nazi–Soviet Pact using the following headings:
   - Reasons
   - Terms
   - Result

Peace, War and Neutrality: Britain, Northern Ireland and Ireland 1932–1949

ANGLO–IRISH RELATIONSHIPS UP TO THE OUTBREAK OF THE SECOND WORLD WAR, SEPTEMBER 1939

IRELAND BEFORE 1932

WHAT YOU NEED TO KNOW

Before looking at developments after 1932, you should gain a little background knowledge of **how** and **why** Ireland was partitioned and what impact partition had.

PARTITION

Northern Ireland was established by the 1920 Government of Ireland Act. This Act partitioned Ireland into two parts governed by separate parliaments:

- a 26-county Southern Ireland (which later became the Irish Free State)
- a six-county Northern Ireland.

The Act gave these parliaments control over areas such as education, health and transport. Westminster would keep responsibility for defence, foreign policy and taxation. **Proportional Representation** (PR) would ensure that the minorities would be properly represented.

IRISH FREE STATE

The terms of the Act were unacceptable to Irish **Republicans**. The Anglo–Irish War which had started in 1919 continued between the **Irish Republican Army (IRA)** and British forces. In July 1921 both sides agreed a ceasefire and began to talk. In December 1921 Sinn Féin, Ireland's largest political party, reached agreement with the British and signed the Anglo–Irish Treaty, establishing the Irish Free State as a **dominion** of the **British Commonwealth**. Not everyone was happy with the terms of the Treaty and Éamon de Valera, a Sinn Féin leader, led the anti-Treaty side in an ultimately unsuccessful Civil War. In 1926 he established a new party, Fianna Fáil. It entered the **Dáil Eireann** in 1927 and by 1928 had become the **official opposition** party.

NORTHERN IRELAND

The Government of Ireland Act delighted **Unionists**, as it gave them control over their own affairs. They lost no time in holding elections for the new parliament and their leader, Sir James Craig (Lord Craigavon from 1927), became Prime Minister.

THE FREE STATE UNDER DE VALERA

WHAT YOU NEED TO KNOW

Once in power, de Valera moved rapidly to put distance between the Free State and Britain. You should be able to explain the **different steps** that he took and **how** they impacted on Anglo–Irish relations.

CEMENTING INDEPENDENCE

Following a general election in March 1932, Fianna Fáil, with the support of the Irish Labour Party, became the Free State's government. De Valera soon moved to change parts of the Anglo–Irish Treaty, removing the links with Britain.

- In November 1932 London recalled the **Governor General** (an official who represented the monarch) as Fianna Fáil ministers were snubbing him. His replacement was a Fianna Fáil politician, Domhnall O'Buachalla.

His powers were limited, he never lived in the Governor General's official residence and he undertook no official duties. In addition, de Valera acted in other ways to undermine the position that O'Buachalla held, and thus play down the Free State's link with the British Crown.

- The Removal of the Oath Act (May 1933) eliminated the Oath of Allegiance to the British Monarch that all members of the Dáil had to swear.
- In May 1933 the Free State Constitution was changed to stop people appealing Irish Court verdicts to the **Privy Council**. In 1935 London challenged these actions before the Privy Council. It ruled that the 1931 **Statute of Westminster** gave de Valera the power to make the changes he was making.
- De Valera used the December 1936 **abdication crisis** to pass the External Relations Act. By this the King's official role within the Free State was ended, even though in legal terms Ireland remained a member of the Commonwealth. As a result of this law, the position of Governor General also ceased to exist.

ACTIVITIES

1. Create a timeline of the key changes in the Irish Free State's relationship with the British Commonwealth, 1932–36.
2. Use the headings below to summarise how de Valera redefined the Irish Free State's relationship with the British Commonwealth:
   - Governor General
   - Oath of allegiance
   - British Privy Council
   - External Relations Act

THE 1937 CONSTITUTION

WHAT YOU NEED TO KNOW

You must be able to explain **what** the key articles of *Bunreacht na hÉireann* were and **how** London and Belfast reacted to them.

BUNREACHT NA HÉIREANN

In 1937 de Valera made an important break with the Irish Free State by introducing a new constitution, *Bunreacht na hÉireann*. It included several significant changes from the 1922 constitution:

1. The Irish Free State would henceforth be known as Éire.
2. The title of the head of government would be ***Taoiseach***.
3. The (mainly ceremonial) head of state would have the title of President. The position would be decided by an election, held every seven years. In 1938 Douglas Hyde, a well-known Gaelic scholar, became the first President of Éire.
4. The green, white and orange tricolour became the national flag.

The Constitution recognised Irish as the official language of the state (English was recognised as the second language). It also said that the Catholic Church would have a 'special position … as the guardian of the faith professed by the great majority of the citizens' although 'freedom of conscience and the free profession and practice of religion' was granted to other faiths. Article II claimed that Dublin had the right to rule over the whole island. However, Article III added that, until the end of partition, Éire's laws would only apply to the 26 counties that were currently controlled by Dublin.

Nowhere in the new constitution could any reference to the King be found. Éire had become a republic in all but name, yet despite this, de Valera did not declare Éire a republic and the country still remained part of the Commonwealth. Speaking in the Dáil on the passage of the new constitution, de Valera suggested that breaking the link with Britain completely would make partition even harder to end.

REACTIONS

Unsure whether Éire remained in the Commonwealth or not, London decided that the changes introduced were relatively unimportant and did not alter its existing relationship with Dublin. Unionists, however, were not so calm. *Bunreacht na hÉireann* reinforced their fears and suspicions of their neighbours and strengthened their determination to remain within the UK.

The Unionist government – located at **Stormont** since 1932 – strongly criticised the new constitution. It condemned Éire's territorial claim over Northern Ireland and denounced the particular mention of the position of the Catholic Church and the Irish language. Lord Craigavon used the opportunity to call a snap general election in 1938, resulting in an increased Unionist majority.

ACTIVITIES

1. Create a spider diagram illustrating the three key constitutional changes made.
2. Analyse the terms of *Bunreacht na hÉireann* using the following headings:
   - Irish language
   - Catholic Church
   - Other faiths
   - Northern Ireland
   - King
   - Commonwealth
3. How did the following groups react to *Bunreacht na hÉireann*?
   - British government
   - Northern Irish government
   - Northern Nationalists

Some historians believe that the introduction of *Bunreacht na hÉireann* also left northern Nationalists dissatisfied. Despite the inclusion of Articles II and III, it could be argued that – by removing almost all links with Britain and the Commonwealth – *Bunreacht na hÉireann* actually strengthened partition and so made reunification even more unlikely.

THE ECONOMIC WAR

LAND ANNUITIES

Land reform had been one of the biggest issues in nineteenth-century Irish history. The 1870 Land Act tried to solve the problem by lending tenants money to buy land. Each year the farmers paid back part of the loan (known as land annuities). Between 1922 and 1932 the money was collected by the Irish government and sent on to London. The payments were worth an estimated £5m per year to the British Government.

Irish farmers – believing that they owned the land – disliked making these payments and following his election, de Valera stopped them. He argued that:

- The Irish economy was suffering from the consequences of a worldwide economic depression and so the money could not be spared.
- The British Government had abolished Northern Ireland's land annuities. Farmers in the Free State should be treated the same.

THE ECONOMIC WAR

Britain responded by imposing **duties** of 20 per cent on Free State imports. The Irish Government took the following measures:

- A snap general election was called in January 1933. This gave de Valera enough seats to rule without the Labour Party, strengthening his position.
- Similar duties on imports from Great Britain and Northern Ireland were imposed.

The standoff (which became known as the Economic War) continued for six years, although in 1935 both sides took a step back by agreeing the Coal–Cattle Pact that made trade in these two essential commodities much easier.

IMPACT ON THE IRISH ECONOMY

As 90 per cent of Irish exports went to Britain, this war had a significant impact.

Farming

Whilst Dublin benefited from being able to keep the £5m previously paid to London, Irish farmers probably suffered most with a 35 per cent reduction in cattle exports (from 1929 levels) resulting in massive beef overproduction and many farmers going bankrupt. Much of this reduction came from a decrease in trade with Britain, however part also resulted from the loss of cross-border trade with Northern Ireland. Alternative markets were unavailable to Irish farmers due to the impact of the ongoing world economic depression. **Subsistence** farmers in Éire probably suffered less during the Economic War as they benefited from the reduction in their annuity payments.

The Irish Government encouraged farmers to explore new markets by offering subsidies to increase production of crops such as sugar beet and wheat. However, this enjoyed limited success as these crops were grown by farmers instead of other more traditional crops such as barley. Moreover, it was only the bigger farmers who made the switch. Smaller-scale farmers

WHAT YOU NEED TO KNOW

Make sure you understand **what** caused the Economic War, **what** form it took, **how** it was ended and **what** impact it had on relations within the British Isles.

ACTIVITIES

1. Analyse the beginning of the Economic War using the following headings:
   - Land annuities before 1922
   - Land annuities 1922–32
   - Why de Valera withheld payment
   - British response
   - Irish response
   - De Valera's hopes for Irish industry
2. Examine the impact of the Economic War by writing a sentence on each of the following areas:
   - Impact on the Irish economy
   - Impact on the British and Northern Irish economies
   - Impact on relations between Britain, Northern Ireland and Ireland

kept on growing traditional crops. As a result, living standards fell even though taxes were raised to compensate farmers. At the same time, small-scale farmers did benefit from the reduction of the land annuity payments, now made to the Dublin Government.

Industry

De Valera hoped that increasing the price of British goods would stop people buying them. He hoped to encourage the development of Irish industries that would produce similar goods more cheaply. This failed to happen, however, mainly due to a lack of investment. In addition, the new Irish industries were not able to sell their products abroad, as they were not geared up for the export market. As a result, the economy experienced a trade deficit as well as cut backs in electricity generation and rail transport. On the other hand, the lack of UK coal imports did result in a period of growth for the local peat industry. In addition, cement factories were established in Drogheda and Limerick, while the Dublin government spent £1 million on improving bridges and rural cottages.

THE BRITISH AND NORTHERN IRISH ECONOMIES

The Economic War led to a deterioration in Dublin's relations with London and Belfast. It is probably fair to say that the War had a much greater impact on Northern Ireland; however, there is some evidence to suggest that unemployment in Britain did increase. That said, while Britain had many other markets for its goods, much of Northern Ireland's economic prosperity had been built on the existence of strong cross-border trade with the Free State. All such trade came to a halt during the six years of the Economic War, although smuggling increased as a method of avoiding the payment of such duties. On the other hand, Northern Ireland's farmers were helped by being given the opportunity to provide Britain with produce no longer being supplied by the Irish Free State.

THE ANGLO–IRISH AGREEMENT OF 1938

Chamberlain decided that in light of growing tensions in Europe (the result of the emergence and growth of **fascism**, Nazism and communism), Anglo–Irish relations needed to improve. This would mean:

- ending the Economic War
- resolving the issue of the treaty ports (three British naval bases in Éire).

Although Chamberlain recognised the strategic value of the ports, he also knew that they were out of date. He therefore decided that returning them would, hopefully; result in Éire's assistance if war broke out. Chamberlain also knew that the Economic War had impacted on employment levels in those British ports which had handled trade from Éire. Ending the War could have a positive impact in these ports.

For his part de Valera was keen to get the ports back. He wanted to safeguard Éire's neutrality in the event of a war and believed that Britain's continued control of the ports would weaken Éire's claims to neutrality and leave her open to attack.

The two governments began to talk in January 1938. In April they signed three separate agreements centred on defence, finance and trade. As a result the Economic War (and the duties imposed during it) was ended – thus improving trade links – and the three treaty ports were returned to Éire (without any specific assurance that Britain would have use of them if there was a war). As a result, another symbolic link between the two countries was broken and Éire's independence was further reinforced. In terms of the specific detail; Éire agreed to pay Britain £10 million to resolve the annuities question, believed to be worth an estimated £78 million, whilst all duties imposed during the Economic War were removed. The end to the trade war did not apply to cross-border trade with Northern Ireland which was subject to a long-running boycott.

WHAT YOU NEED TO KNOW

You must be able to explain the reasons **why** Britain and Éire decided to end their differences and understand the different reactions to their decision.

ACTIVITIES

1. Summarise the different attitudes to the issue of the treaty ports under the following headings:
   - Chamberlain's attitude
   - De Valera's attitude
2. Analyse the Anglo–Irish Agreement under the following headings:
   - Date
   - Key terms
   - Majority response
   - Churchill's response
   - Unionists' response

While the agreements received a generally favourable response, the return of the treaty ports was sharply criticised by Craigavon and Winston Churchill. Churchill did not believe that Éire would allow Britain to use the ports in a war and felt that their return would weaken the security of both nations. Unionists were also fearful that the improvement in Anglo–Irish relations might lead to reunification with Ireland.

BRITAIN AND THE THREAT OF WAR

WHAT YOU NEED TO KNOW

Make sure that you understand **what** appeasement was, **why** it was the option chosen by the British Government and **why** it was ultimately discredited.

TENSIONS IN EUROPE

By the mid-1930s, the risk of war in Europe was growing. Mussolini had already begun a war in Abyssinia in 1935, while Hitler had begun to undo the military restrictions placed on Germany by the Treaty of Versailles. On top of this, Stalin's programme of economic development in the USSR led some to fear that the Soviet Union might also try to spread the influence of communism.

As the risk of war grew, the British government had to choose between neutrality, rearmament or appeasement.

Neutrality

A neutral Britain would not get involved in war. While there were many who supported such a policy, Britain also had to consider that the security of its empire might not be well served by neutrality.

Rearmament

While rearmament would be costly and unpopular at a time of economic crisis, faced with Germany's military expansion; Britain was forced to increase defence spending.

Appeasement

Appeasement meant that Britain (and France) made concessions to their opponents to buy them off. Britain adopted appeasement as its main policy as:

- Her economy was still recovering from the impact of the First World War and the Great Depression and was not able to bear the cost of rapid rearmament.
- People still remembered the brutality of the 1914–18 war.
- Many leaders – particularly British Prime Minister Neville Chamberlain – saw Hitler as a realistic man with sensible demands who could be dealt with by reasonable policies.

ACTIVITIES

1 Create a spider diagram showing why there was increasing unrest in Europe in the mid-1930s.

2 Make a copy of the following table and fill it in:

Reasons appeasement introduced	Reasons appeasement ended	How appeasement benefited Britain

IMPACT

Appeasement allowed Britain to begin to rebuild its military. Improvements were made to the size of the Royal Navy and the Royal Air Force (RAF), which also benefited from reorganisation, the development of modern aircraft and the installation of **radar** stations. The Government also ordered the building of anti-aircraft weapons, searchlights, **barrage balloons** and air raid shelters. Westminster passed the Air Raid Precaution Act, creating Air Raid Protection wardens and making plans for evacuation from London and other cities. In addition, gas masks were provided for the entire population.

Hitler, however, used appeasement to his advantage. While there was no great public opposition to the 1936 German remilitarisation of the Rhineland, the 1938 *Anschluss* with Austria – and particularly Hitler's treatment of Czechoslovakia in 1938 and 1939 – led to appeasement being discredited.

At that late stage Britain and France realised that appeasement had failed and, in April 1939, the two countries offered military guarantees to Poland in an effort to prevent a German attack. Confident that the August 1939 Nazi–Soviet Pact neutralised the USSR as an opponent, Hitler ignored the Anglo–French guarantees and invaded Poland in

September 1939. When Britain's ultimatum to withdraw was ignored, war was declared on 3 September 1939.

RESPONSE OF NORTHERN IRELAND TO THE THREAT OF WAR

CONSCRIPTION

In April 1939 London had announced the introduction of conscription in response to the deteriorating international situation. However, the fear of a negative nationalist reaction and the desire not to worsen relations with Dublin meant that conscription was not extended to Northern Ireland. An irate Craigavon demanded that the decision be reversed.

This demand annoyed Nationalists and the North's Catholic bishops issued a statement opposing Craigavon's appeal. De Valera also voiced his concerns.

Craigavon reluctantly accepted the decision following a meeting with Chamberlain in May 1939.

To compensate, Northern Ireland was awarded over £6 million in defence contracts. Particularly involved were the Short & Harland aircraft factory and the Harland & Wolff shipyard. While this investment resulted in a fall of over 30,000 in unemployment levels during 1939, it also meant that in a war Belfast could be a target for enemy bombers.

In the absence of conscription, Craigavon pushed Westminster to agree to a recruitment drive across Northern Ireland in May 1940. A series of rallies was held across the North; however, the response was not as positive as Craigavon might have hoped. The memories of the carnage of the Battle of the Somme – just 24 years previously – may have played a part in the drive's limited success. Equally limiting – from a nationalist perspective – would have been the choice of the Minister of Agriculture, Sir Basil Brooke, to lead the recruitment campaign. Many still remembered a speech made by Brooke in 1933 when he had urged unionist employers to 'employ good Protestant lads and lassies'.

WHAT YOU NEED TO KNOW

You need to be able to explain the **reasons** for and **reactions** to London's refusal to extend conscription to Northern Ireland.

ACTIVITIES

1. Create a spider diagram on conscription showing (i) Those in favour and (ii) Those against.
2. Make notes about defence production under the following headings:
   - Amount awarded to Northern Ireland companies
   - Companies that benefited
   - Impact on unemployment
   - Dangers for Belfast

THE DECLARATION OF WAR

DECLARATION OF WAR

The outbreak of war resulted in different reactions in Belfast and Dublin.

NORTHERN IRELAND

The war provided the Stormont government with the opportunity to demonstrate its continued loyalty to Great Britain, which had been professed on many previous occasions, including during the 1938 Munich Crisis. In this way its union with the United Kingdom could be strengthened. Speaking during a parliamentary debate on 4 September, Craigavon reassured London of Northern Ireland's readiness to play its part in the forthcoming war effort.

ÉIRE AND NEUTRALITY

On the same date de Valera announced Éire's neutrality. There were a number of reasons for the Éire government's decision to introduce this policy:

- De Valera correctly assumed that the population would support neutrality as another way of reinforcing Éire's independence from Great Britain.
- The continued existence of partition ruled out Éire's involvement in the war.
- The Éire population was divided over whether or not to support the British war effort, indeed some may even have been sympathetic to Germany.
- Many in Éire believed Germany posed no threat to Éire.

WHAT YOU NEED TO KNOW

You need to be able to explain **how** the Belfast and Dublin governments responded to the start of the Second World War.

ACTIVITY

Analyse the different responses to the outbreak of the Second World War under the following headings:

- Belfast reaction
- Dublin reaction

- If such a threat were to emerge, it was believed that Britain would protect Éire, as a member of the Commonwealth.
- Éire was not equipped to fight a war.
- The Dublin government wanted to unite its people against invasion and protect them against the hardships of war.

By and large neutrality was a popular policy. But at the same time the population remained largely sympathetic to the Allied cause. Indeed, de Valera agreed to the appointment of a British representative to Dublin, in order to avoid any misunderstandings with London.

The government also introduced the Emergency Powers Act, increasing its control over the country. This gave the government extensive powers to ensure that the policy of neutrality was maintained. For example, censorship was introduced and strictly enforced.

BRITAIN'S ATTITUDE TOWARDS NORTHERN IRELAND'S SUPPORT AND ÉIRE'S NEUTRALITY

Great Britain accepted Éire's declaration of neutrality only grudgingly. It was viewed in some quarters as being potentially damaging to the war effort while fears were expressed that Germany might use Éire as a base from which to invade Great Britain. Particular opposition came from Winston Churchill, soon to be appointed Prime Minister. Reactions in Northern Ireland were even less positive. North of the border there was strong resentment at Éire's declaration of neutrality which was viewed as an act of betrayal and a threat to the security of the United Kingdom. While there was some improvement in North–South relations when de Valera sent fire engines North during the 1940 Belfast Blitz (see page 31), his protests in relation to the arrival of US troops in Northern Ireland in 1942 were taken as clear evidence of his pro-Nazi sympathies.

The Westminster government's reaction to the support provided by Northern Ireland was much more positive and can be seen in the decision to provide funding for the introduction of the **Welfare State** in the years following the end of the Second World War (see page 38).

THE EFFECTS OF THE SECOND WORLD WAR ON NORTHERN IRELAND AND ÉIRE

READY FOR WAR?

WHAT YOU NEED TO KNOW

Make sure that you can identify the main features of Northern Ireland's preparations for war.

COMPLACENCY?

Northern Ireland was not ready for war and the government was slow to act to make it so. Believing that the province was beyond the range of enemy aircraft, appropriate defence measures (both aerial and ground-based) were not put in place.

It was not until well into 1941 that the majority of the province was covered by radar and steps had been taken to establish anti-aircraft batteries.

With the German defeat of France in June 1940, the possibility of air attack increased. This led to a significant reorganisation of the RAF which included:

- an increase in the number of RAF squadrons within Northern Ireland
- the provision of up-to-date Hurricane fighter aircraft
- the construction of airfields in location such as Aldergrove and Ballykelly.

While this improved the RAF's ability to protect Northern Ireland, it remained too poorly resourced to be able to defend the province completely.

PREPARED FOR ENEMY ATTACK?

Nor did Northern Ireland compare well to the wide-ranging evacuation and air raid protection schemes implemented across Britain prior to the outbreak of war:

- Stormont introduced an Air Raid Precautions Act in 1938; however, unlike the rest of the UK, it did not make local council provision of civil defence measures compulsory.
- Public responses to the dangers of air attack were also unacceptable. Air Raid Protection (ARP) wardens, who had the job of enforcing blackouts, were not taken seriously and blackouts were routinely ignored.
- By early 1941, recorded blackout offences in Belfast had reached nearly 1,000 per month.
- When people were offered the chance to be evacuated from Belfast in case of air raids, few went.
- When Belfast was bombed in 1941 (see page 31), there weren't enough recruits for the various civil defence services.
- In spite of constant advice and warnings, the majority of people did not carry gas masks until after the Belfast Blitz.
- It was not until July 1940 that a local evacuation plan was launched and even this only resulted in 10 per cent of children being evacuated.
- Nearly a year after the declaration of war only 15 per cent of the Belfast households entitled to an Anderson air raid shelter had received one.

MACDERMOTT'S REFORMS

With the appointment of John MacDermott as Minister of Public Security in June 1940, things began to improve a little. He organised:

- the rapid erection of public air raid shelters
- the reinforcement of the emergency services
- efforts to evacuate children from Belfast.

At the same time, blackout curtains were used to stop lights alerting *Luftwaffe* pilots of the locations of towns and cities across Northern Ireland.

However, when the *Luftwaffe* bombed Belfast in April and May 1941, the city still only had 22 anti-aircraft guns, insufficient air cover from fighter aircraft and public shelters capable of housing no more than a quarter of the city's population.

ACTIVITY

Examine Northern Ireland's preparation for war, 1939–41, under the following headings:

- Positive developments
- Areas of concern

THE BATTLE OF BRITAIN

WHAT YOU NEED TO KNOW

The Battle of Britain was a crucial early moment in the war. Make sure that you are clear about **why** it happened and **why** the RAF was ultimately victorious.

PREPARING FOR WAR

By the end of June 1940 Britain stood alone against Germany; however, her army lacked both the numbers and the equipment needed to defend her from invasion. Steps were swiftly taken to address this situation:

- Factories worked multiple shifts to produce aircraft, tanks and heavy weapons. Their efforts were boosted by the introduction of a government campaign for scrap metal from Britain's households.
- Over 500,000 rifles were ordered from the USA.
- The Local Defence Volunteers (later renamed the Home Guard) was set up in May 1940. In just over a year it had more than 1 million members.

Although the Royal Navy had begun a blockade of the North Sea and was patrolling the Channel to defend against German warships and U-boats, the RAF was in a stronger position due to the programme of improvements that had been ongoing since 1935. Radar provided advance warning of the approach of enemy aircraft and also enabled RAF fighters to be directed accurately to intercept enemy planes. In addition, the RAF was reorganised into three sections:

- Fighter Command
- Bomber Command
- Coastal Command

Britain's preparations for war included the development of a civil defence plan consisting of:

- mass evacuation plans for women and children
- the distribution of gas masks
- the provision of 400,000 Anderson air raid shelters
- the establishment of the ARP.

BATTLE FOR THE SKIES

In July 1940 Hitler ordered the implementation of Operation Sealion, the invasion of Britain. Before this could take place, however, the RAF would have to be destroyed as its control of the skies would prevent a successful sea invasion.

On 12 August 1940 the *Luftwaffe* launched Operation Eagle, its attack on the RAF. This was two months later than originally planned, giving the RAF time to increase its fighter plane numbers from 446 to 704. Although initial *Luftwaffe* losses were greater (225 aircraft losses against the RAF's 117), it still had significantly more aircraft and so it is likely that if these attacks had continued, the RAF would eventually have been worn down. However, on 7 September the *Luftwaffe* switched tactics in response to recent RAF raids on Berlin and started to bomb London. These raids continued for months and soon included other British cities such as Coventry, Liverpool and Glasgow.

While the nightly blitz caused massive devastation to cities and Britain's civilian population, the change of tactics allowed the RAF to reorganise and obtain newly manufactured aircraft. This meant that it continued to control the skies over Britain and for this reason Operation Sealion was finally called off in October 1940.

ACTIVITIES

1. Create a spider diagram illustrating the different ways that Britain prepared for war.
2. Analyse the **Battle of Britain** using the following headings:
   - Reasons for the start of the Battle of Britain
   - Different stages
   - Outcome

THE BELFAST BLITZ

WHAT YOU NEED TO KNOW

There are three key aspects of the Belfast Blitz for you to understand:

1. **Why** it happened.
2. Its **impact** on lives, property and industry.
3. Its **political impact.**

TARGETING BELFAST

In 1941 Belfast was targeted by over 150 *Luftwaffe* bombers. This was because:

- Germany was aware of the key role that some of the city's industries were playing in the war effort
- Northern Ireland was playing an important strategic role in the war.

The *Luftwaffe* visited Belfast four times in 1941 (7–8 April, 15–16 April, 4–5 May and 5–6 May). As a result:

- The city's most densely populated areas were targeted. As a consequence 955 civilians were killed, and 2,436 were injured.
- Almost 57,000 homes – more than 50 per cent of the total number – were damaged or destroyed, leaving over 100,000 people temporarily homeless and 15,000 permanently so. In addition, two hospitals, two schools and eleven places of worship were also destroyed by *Luftwaffe* bombs.
- In the short term many thousands fled Belfast to the rest of Northern Ireland and even to Éire, enduring harsh conditions in the process.
- Belfast's industrial infrastructure, the bombers' main target, suffered extensive damage. Indeed no British shipyard suffered greater damage during a single raid than Harland and Wolff did as a consequence of the raid of 4-5 May 1941. As a result it took six months for industrial production to recover.

Relatively speaking, Belfast suffered more from *Luftwaffe* attacks than other British cities had up to that point. The 745 deaths that resulted from the raid of 15–16 April was greater than the number of deaths resulting from a single raid elsewhere in the United Kingdom. This was because:

- Belfast had the lowest proportion of air-raid shelters of any city in the United Kingdom.

ACTIVITIES

1. Analyse the Belfast Blitz using the following headings:
   - Reasons
   - Impact
   - Results
2. For Craigavon and Andrews note down the following information:
   - Dates in office
   - Reason for appointment
   - Reason for leaving office
3. Why was Brooke appointed as the new Prime Minister?

- No searchlights were set up, as they only arrived on April 10.
- There were no night-fighters patrolling the skies over Northern Ireland.
- There were only 22 anti-aircraft guns in position.
- There was no smokescreen ability.
- There were only a relatively small number of barrage balloons above Belfast and during the Blitz they were too low to hinder the *Luftwaffe*.
- Measures to protect the civilian population were poor. For example, extra fire engines were almost impossible to obtain because of the demands of English cities for such protection.
- Unlike other main British cities, children had not been evacuated in significant numbers. Evacuation plans had only ever been drawn up in the vaguest form and when the *Luftwaffe* attacked, the thousands who fled the city had nowhere in particular to go. As many as 10,000 ended up crossing the border into Éire and thousands of others left to stay with family and friends in provincial towns.

Above all, the failure of the Northern Ireland government to take seriously the threat that Belfast and other areas faced from the *Luftwaffe* and thus to put in place an effective defence plan meant that Northern Ireland's capital city suffered grievously from the impact of the Blitz. It was only in the aftermath of the Blitz that Belfast's air defences were strengthened and additional air raid shelters constructed.

Other parts of Northern Ireland also suffered, although not on the same scale. Derry/Londonderry was also raided in April 1941. The bombs fell on civilian housing in the city's Pennyburn area, killing 15 people. Also attacked were Bangor (where five civilians lost their lives) and Newtownards Airport (where ten guards died).

LEADERSHIP CHANGES

The Blitz highlighted the dreadful conditions that many of Belfast's citizens were living in as well as the bad job that the government was making of the war effort. Upon his death in 1940, Craigavon had been replaced as Prime Minister by his Finance Minister, J.M. Andrews. Unfortunately, Andrews was not up to the demands of the job, yet he obstinately refused to make up for his own shortcomings by promoting younger, more able ministers.

Despite its loyalty to the Unionist Party, Northern Ireland's voting public showed its verdict at the ballot box. In 1942 two seats were lost in **by-elections**. By 1943 there were growing complaints about the quality of leadership on offer. Faced with the threatened resignation of his two most able ministers, Basil Brooke and J.C. MacDermott (along with up to four others), Andrews resigned in April 1943. Brooke became the new Prime Minister.

NORTHERN IRELAND'S WAR EFFORT (I): STRATEGIC

WHAT YOU NEED TO KNOW

There are several different aspects to Northern Ireland's strategic role in the war. Make sure that you can comment in detail on the different roles that it played.

CONSCRIPTION AGAIN

In the aftermath of the Belfast Blitz, the British Labour Minister, Ernest Bevin, again raised the possibility of conscription for Northern Ireland. De Valera condemned the proposal, while thousands of Nationalists – supported by local Catholic bishops and Nationalist politicians – marched in protest in Belfast.

The strength of opposition meant that the Unionist leadership, after initially welcoming Bevin's idea, realised that introducing it would create more problems than it would solve. Moreover, the RUC Inspector-General informed the government of his fear that introducing conscription could lead to serious public disorder. Once again, the idea was shelved.

MILITARY SERVICE

Many Irish people still fought in the war though.

- It is estimated that close to 40,000 people from Northern Ireland joined one of the services. Just over 10 per cent died. It is probable that more of Northern Ireland's Unionist population would have joined up were it not for the fact that they were employed in **reserved occupations**.
- Many of those who joined up served with considerable distinction. One such individual was James Magennis, a Royal Navy sailor who was awarded the **Victoria Cross** for the part he played in sinking a Japanese cruiser off Borneo.
- In excess of 43,000 Irish citizens fought for the Allies. Their reasons ranged from support of the Allied cause to desperation to escape from poverty. However, the recent history of poor Anglo–Irish relations meant that their contribution was not recognised at home.

The Home Guard

Northern Ireland's experience of the Home Guard differed markedly from Britain's. Craigavon's fear of Republican infiltration if the force was created through open enrolment meant that the **B Specials** formed the core of the local Home Guard. Unlike Britain, the force came under the control of the RUC rather than the army.

As a result Catholic membership was limited and the Home Guard came to be seen as little more than a **sectarian** force.

The Home Guard spent much of its time counteracting the IRA threat. Pro-German sentiments were evident in some Republican circles and, when the war began, the government responded by introducing **internment** to deal with IRA suspects. After several additional moves against Republican suspects – including the arrest of IRA Chief of Staff Hugh McAteer in 1942 – IRA activity dropped off.

STRATEGIC SIGNIFICANCE

Northern Ireland played a key strategic role in the war because of its geographical position. The return of the treaty ports to Éire in 1938 and that country's declaration of neutrality in 1939 increased Northern Ireland's value. It was further increased following the fall of France in June 1940 as Allied shipping began to go north of Ireland (the so-called Western Approaches).

- Naval bases, such as Lisahally outside Derry/Londonderry, provided vital support and services for those vessels involved in the Battle of the Atlantic and acted as bases for ships and submarines keeping sea lanes open. The port at Derry/Londonderry was the biggest base in the United Kingdom for warships protecting merchant ships, and 43 German U-boats surrendered here at the end of the war.
- Derry/Londonderry became an important base for service personnel, including large numbers from the United States and other Allied countries. By mid-1943 there were nearly 150 ships based at the port while by the end of the same year there were an estimated 40,000 military personnel in and around the city.
- Natural inlets such as Lough Foyle provided refuge from U-boat attack for merchant shipping on their trans-Atlantic journeys.
- Air bases such as Aldergrove, Ballykelly, Eglinton, Limavady, Nutts Corner, Long Kesh and Castle Archdale (for Coastal Command) provided much needed cover for **convoys**. Castle Archdale was particularly significant; it provided an extra 100 miles of air cover over the existing base at Loch Ryan in Scotland. Aircraft from Castle Archdale sank 18 U-boats in 1943. Indeed the German warship, Bismarck was sunk by planes using Castle Archdale as a base.
- A variety of US forces used Northern Ireland between 1942 and 1944. Apart from training troops, bases to service aircraft and shipping were

ACTIVITIES

1. Analyse the 1941 conscription crisis using the headings:
   - Those in favour
   - Those against
2. Create a spider diagram illustrating how Ireland (North and South) contributed to the Allies' military campaign.
3. Assess the Northern Ireland Home Guard under the following headings:
   - How recruited (compared with Britain)
   - Why recruited in this way
   - How commanded (compared with Britain)
   - Catholic attitude to and involvement in the Home Guard
4. Create a spider diagram illustrating Northern Ireland's strategic importance to the war effort.

established. Most notable among these service bases was Langford Lodge on the shores of Lough Neagh. Magee College in Derry/Londonderry served as the main communication base for US forces across Europe.

- Northern Ireland was also used as a base for preparations for operations in North Africa, Southern Italy and for D-Day. By 1943 there were close to 300,000 military personnel stationed throughout the province. One unforeseen consequence of such huge numbers was that there was sometimes friction with the local male population, unhappy at the 'challenge' of those in uniform!

NORTHERN IRELAND'S WAR EFFORT (II): ECONOMIC

WHAT YOU NEED TO KNOW

There are two key aspects of Northern Ireland's economic war effort that you need to understand. Make sure that you can comment on areas of **success** and **failure**.

AGRICULTURE

The best-performing section of the wartime economy was agriculture. With increasing demand in Britain for food, the amount of land used for growing crops increased by 60 per cent as farmers switched from livestock to arable farming. Particularly significant were the increases in the production of flax, oats and potatoes. The number of allotments increased fourfold. Careful planning by the government ensured that sufficient artificial fertilisers were made available to support this increase which became known as the 'Dig for victory'. There were significant increases in the number of cattle and poultry. The latter were responsible for providing Britain with 20 per cent of its egg consumption. Northern Ireland also exported sheep, cattle and dairy produce (£3 million-worth per year); Scotland received 100,000 litres of Northern Ireland milk each day. As a result farmers grew wealthy.

There were two main reasons for this remarkable performance:

1. Continued availability of fertilisers.
2. The more than one hundred-fold increase in tractor numbers.

Much of the credit for the success of the agricultural sector belongs to the Minister for Agriculture, Basil Brooke. He took to the countryside to persuade Northern Ireland's farmers to increase production. His success played no small part in his appointment as Prime Minister in 1943.

ACTIVITIES

1. Examine Northern Ireland's agricultural performance using the following headings:
   - Examples of improvement
   - Reasons for improvement
2. Create a spider diagram illustrating the impact of rationing on Northern Ireland.
3. Examine Northern Ireland's industrial performance using the following headings:
   - Areas of success
   - Areas of failure

RATIONING

The war resulted in the introduction of rationing to discourage waste and encourage self-reliance. The Department of Agriculture became responsible for the purchase, distribution and sale of food throughout Northern Ireland. By 1941 goods such as fresh meat and dairy produce had become difficult to source, particularly in towns. Sugar, tea and imported fruits also became scarce; however pork, bacon and vegetables were not rationed. Fuel shortages had a massive impact on car use and the use of public transport increased, particularly travel by rail which was not hampered by the rationing of petrol as trains used coal. The lack of petrol meant that milkmen had to give up their floats and employ the horse and cart for their deliveries. For some, particularly those close to the border, smuggling eased the shortages; others resorted to the black market.

INDUSTRY

For the first two years of the war industrial output was hit by:

- bad management
- a lack of planning (by early 1941 no new factories had been built)
- a shortage of skilled workers coupled with questionable working practices
- a series of strikes (even though they were supposed to be illegal).

Although things began to pick up in late 1941, it was really 1943 before industrial output really improved. After initially increasing, unemployment dropped from a high of 70,000 (late 1941) to just 10,000. Production figures began an upward climb and wages and living standards improved. A variety of Northern Ireland firms produced a significant number of tanks, ships, aircraft and munitions. This is best illustrated by looking at how two of Northern Ireland's largest companies performed during the war years:

- Harland & Wolff:
  - 140 warships (including three destroyers and six aircraft carriers)
  - 123 merchant ships (10% of the UK's total wartime production)
  - 3,000 ships repaired or converted to other uses
  - 500 tanks
  - over 13 million aircraft components.

Harland & Wolff was also responsible for running the Foyle Yard in Derry/Londonderry which served as a repair base for Atlantic convoy escorts.

- Short & Harland:
  - 1,500 Stirling bombers
  - 125 Sunderland flying boats
  - 150 Hereford bombers
  - over 3,000 aircraft repairs.

Other companies produced wartime essentials including weapons and ammunition (especially James Mackie and Sons), nets and ropes, as well as uniforms and parachutes. In total, local factories produced close to 75,000 shells, 180 million bullets, 50,000 bayonets, 50,000 camouflage/cargo nets, 30,000 shirts, 200,000 yards of cloth (for uniforms), 2 million flax cloth parachutes and 250,000 tons of rope (one third of the total amount of rope used by the British Army). While these figures are impressive, historical research would suggest that Northern Ireland's economic performance might still have been better.

THE SECOND WORLD WAR AND ÉIRE (I): MILITARY PREPARATIONS

Despite de Valera's declaration of neutrality, there remained the possibility that Germany might invade Éire as the first stage of an invasion of Britain. This possibility – discussed by representatives of both governments – also made it likely that British Army units based in Northern Ireland would move into Éire to secure its vulnerable western flanks.

Well aware of the limitations of its armed services, the government extended the defence forces by:

- Increasing the size of the army to over 40,000.
- Creating a reserve force in the shape of the Local Defence Force. However, this force of 250,000 was poorly equipped.
- Extending the size of the navy.
- Establishing an air force.

THE IRA

De Valera moved against the IRA following its rather clumsy efforts to conspire with Germany and because its members had stolen 1 million rounds of ammunition from a Dublin magazine. Using the Offences Against the State Act, internment was implemented against at least 1,000 suspected IRA members. Six IRA members were hanged in 1942 and when a further three went on hunger strike, nothing was done to prevent their deaths. De Valera's stance was supported by the vast majority of the population. The government's onslaught left the IRA broken.

WHAT YOU NEED TO KNOW

You must be clear about how Éire responded to the start of the Second World War. In particular you need to be able to explain **what** military changes were introduced.

ACTIVITIES

1. Analyse the Dublin government's response to the threat of invasion under the following headings:
   - Invitation to Britain for assistance
   - Defence forces
2. Examine de Valera's actions against the IRA using the following headings:
   - Reasons
   - Actions
   - Outcomes

THE SECOND WORLD WAR AND ÉIRE (II): ASSESSING NEUTRALITY

WHAT YOU NEED TO KNOW

You must be clear about **how** neutrality operated in practice and **how** it impacted on Anglo–Irish relations.

JOINING THE WAR?

After Winston Churchill became Prime Minister in May 1940, Britain made two main attempts to encourage Ireland on to her side:

- In June 1940 London proposed reunification if Éire joined the Allies. In return the Dublin government would allow British forces to be stationed in Éire and use naval facilities. However, de Valera rejected the offer on the strength of Éire's 'unpreparedness', the negative impact it would have on independence and the fact that there was no guarantee that Northern Ireland would agree as its government had not been consulted.
- Following the Japanese attack on Pearl Harbor (7 December 1941), Churchill telegrammed de Valera. His offer of 'Now is your chance. Now or never "A nation once again"', was understood by de Valera to refer to the possibility of Irish unity if he joined the Allies. Again he declined.

In 1942 Churchill attempted to regain the use of the treaty ports. Once again his efforts were rejected.

TOTALLY NEUTRAL?

Éire asserted its neutrality during the war in a number of ways:

- It refused military assistance to both sides.
- The Allies were denied use of Éire's ports and airfields.
- News bulletins gave purely factual reports about the war.
- Weather forecasts ceased to be broadcast in case they helped either side.
- De Valera resisted US pressure to end neutrality when the US entered the war in late 1941.

De Valera went to great lengths to display even-handedness. He irritated Washington by protesting at the arrival of US troops in Northern Ireland in 1942. He outraged Allied opinion in April 1945 when he expressed sympathy over Hitler's death. He had, however, similarly regretted the death of US President, Franklin D. Roosevelt.

Frequently, however, Dublin's actions made it appear that their neutrality was biased in favour of the Allies:

- The German ambassador's radio transmitter was confiscated.
- German pilots who bailed out over Éire were imprisoned while Allied airmen were allowed to cross the border into Northern Ireland.
- During the Belfast Blitz, de Valera sent 13 fire engines (with 71 crew) to help. In its aftermath, relief centres were set up close to the border, relief funds were started and officials from both governments met to discuss how best the refugee problem could be handled.
- Allied airmen patrolling the Western Approaches or refuelling on trans-Atlantic missions were permitted to fly over Irish territory via the 'Donegal Air Corridor' (from Belleek to the coast). Later in the war, US airmen were also permitted to use this route.
- Coastal navigational aids were provided for US airmen.
- In the final months of the war, de Valera allowed the RAF to establish a number of secret radar bases on Irish territory.

WHOSE CREDIT?

It is important to consider the real reasons for Éire's ability to remain neutral.

- Éire benefited from the sympathetic attitude of the British and German representatives in Dublin, and their recommendations to their respective governments not to do anything that would compromise that neutrality.

ACTIVITIES

1. Using the following headings, write a summary of Churchill's attempts to get Éire to join the Allies in the Second World War and de Valera's response:
   - Date
   - Churchill's actions
   - De Valera's response
2. Create a spider diagram showing how Éire's neutrality was biased towards the Allies.
3. What part did the following play in Éire's successful maintenance of neutrality during the war?
   - German and British ambassadors
   - Northern Ireland

- If the Allies had found it strategically necessary to invade the South there is little doubt that they would have done so. That they did not was due mainly to the significant strategic role that Northern Ireland played during the conflict.

This possibility of an Allied invasion was revealed in a speech Churchill made when the war ended, in which he condemned de Valera's inaction. At the same time Churchill praised the part played by Northern Ireland, which prevented Great Britain from having 'to come to close quarters with Mr de Valera, or perish forever from the earth'.

In his reply de Valera asked Churchill if he could not 'find in his heart the generosity to acknowledge that there is a small nation that stood alone, not for one year or two, but for several hundred years against aggression?'

THE IMPACT OF 'THE EMERGENCY'

The war – or 'Emergency' as it was called – impacted on life in Éire in a number of ways:

- Poor *Luftwaffe* navigation resulted in Dublin being bombed several times. In one attack in May 1941, 28 people died (some historians put the fatalities at 34 while a recent account puts the death-toll at over 40), at least 90 were injured (again, estimates vary) and hundreds of houses were damaged.
- The Ministry of Supplies was set up under Sean Lemass to ensure that Ireland had essential materials. Lemass established the Irish Shipping Company to carry supplies previously brought by British ships. However, factories still had to close because they could not get hold of sufficient natural resources or manufacturing equipment. Petrol and coal were in particularly short supply. As a result of the lack of the latter (which impacted on electricity supplies), the use of turf increased many times over.
- Ireland benefited from a food surplus. However, the lack of available artificial fertilisers (imports from Great Britain dried up by 1942) damaged productivity even if more than one and a half times more land was being used to grow crops. In addition, other imports such as tea and sugar had to be rationed due to the lack of imports. Attempts were made to increase wheat production to support the production of bread. By 1945 over twice as much land was being used for this purpose. Unfortunately the Irish climate was not best suited to this crop. The lack of artificial fertilisers also had an impact. For these reasons rationing had to be introduced.
- The lack of maize meant that home-grown grain had to be used to feed livestock.
- Other goods to be rationed included tea and sugar while fruit and chocolate became unavailable. As a result cross-border smuggling increased while a black market emerged. That said, the availability of most meat and dairy produce (and the potato) meant that most people were able to survive without having to tighten their belts too much.
- The closure of factories had an impact on employment and many Irish people began to seek their fortunes in Britain. It is estimated that between 1939 and 1945 about 200,000 (estimates vary) Irish people emigrated to Britain. Many of these emigrants worked in British munitions factories.
- Inflation increased while wages were kept down by the government. The fall in living standards impacted on the poor in particular. As a result diseases such as tuberculosis (TB) became more common.

At the same time there were no wartime blackouts in Éire and the state's cinemas and theatres remained open for business. As a consequence, large numbers of servicemen and better-off northerners crossed the border for entertainment and nights out.

Despite the population's general support for neutrality, harsh conditions meant that Fianna Fáil lost ten seats in the 1943 general election. Within a year all but one of these seats had been regained in another election.

WHAT YOU NEED TO KNOW

Make sure that you can explain to the examiners **how** life in Éire was affected by the Second World War.

ACTIVITY

Assess the impact of the war on Éire using the following headings:

- Bombing
- Industry
- Agriculture
- Rationing
- Employment and emigration
- Support for Fianna Fáil

POST-WAR SOCIAL AND POLITICAL CHANGES

THE WELFARE STATE (I): GREAT BRITAIN

LABOUR IN POWER

In May 1945 the Second World War ended in Europe; two months later the Labour Party, led by Clement Attlee, won the British general election. Voters were attracted by Labour's promises of jobs for all, government ownership of Britain's industries and, most importantly of all, the introduction of a free healthcare, education and benefits system. This scheme was based on ideas first developed by Lord Beveridge in 1942 and would become known as the Welfare State.

As a result the National Health Service (NHS) came into operation in July 1948. At first it faced opposition from those in the middle and upper classes concerned about the costs in terms of increased taxation, and from doctors fearing that it would limit their freedoms, impact on their ability to earn money and turn them into glorified civil servants. In the end, however, the NHS was joined by 90 per cent of doctors and was hugely successful – even if hugely expensive – and greatly benefited public health in Britain.

WHAT YOU NEED TO KNOW

The introduction of the Welfare State was a major turning point in the history of the United Kingdom. You need to be able to explain **why** it was introduced and **how** it worked.

ACTIVITIES

1 Why did Labour win the 1945 general election?

2 Explain the implementation of the NHS.

THE WELFARE STATE (II): NORTHERN IRELAND

REFORMS IN NORTHERN IRELAND

Despite the need for massive reforms in healthcare and housing following years of poverty and deprivation, many in Northern Ireland worried about what Labour's policies might mean for them. The middle classes and doctors voiced the same objections as their equivalents had done across the Irish Sea. Business leaders feared the implications of nationalisation. Stormont feared the loss of power to a centralising socialist government and wondered how it was to finance such reforms. Not surprisingly, the less well-off welcomed the Welfare State as it promised improvements in their quality of life, while Nationalists welcomed the initiative as they viewed a Labour government as potentially more sympathetic to their situation.

The Labour government demonstrated its gratitude for Northern Ireland's contribution to the war effort by helping to cover the cost of the introduction of the Welfare State through the provision of generous subsidies. In 1948 the NHS came in to operation and the following year saw improvements in a range of areas including:

- family allowance
- national assistance
- the health service (including highly successful campaigns against diseases such as polio and TB: by 1962 Northern Ireland's death rate was the lowest in the UK; in 1939 it had had the highest)
- non-contributing pensions.

At the same time the reforms did mean that Stormont came to rely more and more on the British government for money.

An already serious housing shortage was made worse by the impact of the war. A report commissioned by Brooke after he became Prime Minister estimated that 37 per cent of homes in Belfast were uninhabitable and more than 100,000 new homes were required across Northern Ireland. In 1945 the Northern Ireland Housing Trust was established to oversee their construction. One such scheme was completed at the Woodlands in Guilford, Co, Down; another at Rathcoole on the outskirts of Belfast and another in the Creggan area of Derry/Londonderry. Local councils were also encouraged to build houses through the provision of subsidies; however, they were not as successful. In addition, discrepancies in how council houses were allocated meant that not all benefited equally.

WHAT YOU NEED TO KNOW

The Welfare State also impacted on Northern Ireland. You need to be able to explain the initial fears expressed, **what** was reformed and **how** well it worked.

ACTIVITIES

1 Analyse the background to the introduction of the Welfare State using the following headings:
   - Economic concerns
   - Political concerns

2 Analyse the reforms introduced in Northern Ireland under the following headings:
   - NHS
   - Housing
   - Education
   - Economy

Radical changes were also introduced to the education sector by the 1947 Education Act when the school-leaving age was raised to 15 (with transfer to post-primary education at the age of 11). For the first time children could stay at school free of charge until they were 15. In addition, children who passed the 11+ examination could attend grammar schools, again without payment. As a result the numbers of students in post-primary education doubled over the following years. In addition, local education authorities were required to provide a number of free services to all schools including transport, milk, meals, books, stationery and healthcare. A number of new schools were constructed to cope with the massively increased numbers in education while funding for the voluntary sector increased 65 per cent (much higher than equivalent grants in England). Scholarships were also provided to allow increased numbers to access third level education. Teacher training provision was also improved in both Catholic and Protestant sectors.

Despite lower levels of financial support, the Catholic population gained considerably from these reforms. In spite of the poverty from which they came, increased numbers of Catholic children were able to access secondary and university-level education. As a result of the 1947 Education Act the educational system in Northern Ireland was modernised, even if the old religious divisions remained and were, in many senses, deepened.

The Stormont government also made efforts to improve Northern Ireland's economy, particularly given the long-term decline in some traditional industries such as linen and shipbuilding. The Industrial Development Act (1945) provided the land and incentives for the building of new factories.

ÉIRE: POST-WAR PROBLEMS

DEPRESSION

Post 1945 Éire found itself isolated economically, particularly by Britain and her allies. The reason was their dissatisfaction with Éire's wartime neutrality. The result of this isolation was a severe economic depression, made worse by poor weather in 1946 and 1947:

- Unemployment shot up.
- Building materials, particularly timber, became almost unobtainable so houses could not be built.
- The lack of fertilisers meant that the land was short of essential nutrients, limiting productivity.
- Bad weather in the summer of 1946 led to a further fall in crop production.
- Britain withheld coal imports, resulting in a severe shortage and requiring some trains to now run on oil.
- Éire experienced severe fuel shortages in 1947 as a result of increased demand during the harsh winter weather.
- Wartime rationing remained in force and was extended to include bread from the start of 1947.
- Inflation began to rise and as workers failed to achieve sufficient wage increases, a wave of strikes broke out.
- Emigration rates remained high with as many as 24,000 leaving Éire each year. This in itself had a significant economic impact.

By 1947, the situation had deteriorated to the point where de Valera declared that Éire remained in a state of emergency. Unlike Northern Ireland, state benefits (unemployment, family allowance) were almost non-existent and there was no Welfare State. Instead people had to pay for their medical care. In addition, there was no equivalent of the Housing Trust south of the border.

The outcome was increased unpopularity for the Fianna Fáil government and, as a result, it lost the 1948 general election.

WHAT YOU NEED TO KNOW

The first change of government in 16 years was a major development in Éire. Make sure that you can explain **why** this happened and identify the different groups in the new administration. Be clear as well about the new government's policy initiatives and their impact on the country's social and economic development.

THE INTER-PARTY GOVERNMENT

Following Fianna Fáil's defeat, a coalition government took power. This government was made up of a range of political parties:

- Fine Gael was the largest party. It was set up in 1933 as a union of a number of parties including **Cumann na nGaedheal**.
- There were two different and antagonistic Labour parties.
- Farmers were represented by Clann na Talmhan.
- Clann na Poblachta was a republican and socialist party. It was led by Seán MacBride who had been Chief of Staff of the IRA from 1936 to 1938.
- The government also had the support of twelve independent **TDs**.

As Fine Gael leader, General Richard Mulcahy should have become *Taoiseach*. However, he was unacceptable to MacBride because of his role in the Irish Civil War. For this reason Fine Gael's John A. Costello was appointed as *Taoiseach*.

REFORMS

The new government introduced measures designed to modernise the Irish economy, including:

- The establishment in 1949 of the Industrial Development Authority (IDA). Its purpose was to revitalise Éire's economy.
- The creation of *Córas Tráchtála* to increase trade with North America.
- A house-building programme which resulted in the building of close to 12,000 new houses annually by 1950.
- The signing of a trade agreement with Britain in 1948. This improved profit margins for Irish agricultural exports.

As a result, the Irish economy entered into a slow if steady period of improvement; however, the government's failure to engage in longer-term economic planning meant that the economy did not develop as quickly as it might. At the same time, the problem of emigration continued to bleed away the potential of the Irish population.

ACTIVITIES

1. Create a spider diagram to illustrate the post-war problems in Irish society and in the Irish economy.
2. Create a spider diagram to explain the different groups involved in the Inter-Party Government.
3. List the steps that this government took to try and improve the Irish economy.

ÉIRE BECOMES A REPUBLIC

WHAT YOU NEED TO KNOW

It is important that you can explain **why** a Republic was declared, **how** different groups reacted to it and **what** impact it had on partition.

REASONS

The members of the Inter-Party government – particularly Clann na Poblachta – felt that the 1937 constitution had made Éire a republic in all but name and had left the country neither fully in nor fully out of the Commonwealth. Therefore, in November 1948 the Republic of Ireland Bill was introduced into the Dáil. It came into effect on Easter Monday 1949.

REACTIONS

As Éire was the first country to leave the Commonwealth there was concern about Britain's reaction. If London responded negatively it could have a major impact on the Irish economy and on the position of Irish people living and working in Britain. However, Australia and Canada supported Éire, stating that there was no reason why an Irish Republic could not continue to work closely with the Commonwealth.

London agreed and, while Attlee expressed his sadness at the decision, his government decided that it would not treat Éire as a foreign country but as a near neighbour with a special relationship.

As a result:

- Passports were not needed for travel between the two countries.
- Working permits were not required for Irish workers in the United Kingdom or British workers in the Republic of Ireland.
- Citizens of both nations had voting rights in each other's elections.
- Éire would continue to enjoy preferential treatment compared to non-Commonwealth countries when it came to trade.

ACTIVITIES

1. Analyse reactions to the Declaration of the Republic of Ireland, 1949 under the following headings:
   - Dublin's reasons
   - Commonwealth reaction
   - British reaction
   - Unionist reaction
   - Nationalist reaction
2. Examine the 1949 Ireland Act under the following headings:
   - Reasons
   - Terms
   - Reactions

Reactions to developments in Dublin were mixed north of the border:

- Northern Nationalists unsuccessfully demanded seats in the Dáil so that their views could be heard. Many of them felt abandoned by Dublin and objected to the Inter-Party government's claim that it represented the whole island. Some continued to call the Republic the Irish Free State, believing that the former term should be reserved for a 32-county Irish Republic.
- Unionists felt threatened by the declaration of the Republic. Fearing – correctly – that the Republic would now make a determined effort to reunite Ireland, Unionists rejected Dublin's offers of any reasonable constitutional guarantees if they were to agree to end partition.

Instead the Stormont government pledged its defiance to the declaration of the Republic and used the border issue as the justification for calling a general election for February 1949. Brooke urged Unionists to vote in support of Northern Ireland's continued membership of the United Kingdom. The election became known as the 'chapel gate election'. This was because the money to allow a high number of Nationalist candidates – representing the Anti-Partition League – to stand was raised mainly through collections outside churches in the South. This fact alone caused great resentment within the Unionist community.

The result – after a bitter campaign marred by **sectarian** violence – was an increased share of votes and seats for both sides. Brooke used his increased support to demand a British guarantee of Northern Ireland's future within the United Kingdom.

THE IRELAND ACT

Westminster's response was the Ireland Act of June 1949. It stated that 'In no event will Northern Ireland … cease to be part of … the United Kingdom without the consent of the parliament of Northern Ireland'. Put simply, the Northern Ireland parliament had been given the final word in any future debate about the ending of partition. Unionists felt reassured by these guarantees.

Dublin and Northern Ireland's Nationalists, on the other hand, were outraged and strongly expressed their displeasure with the Act. However, nothing was changed; Attlee felt that as Dublin had not consulted him about the declaration of the Republic, he was free to give whatever guarantees he wanted to Northern Ireland.

Changing Relationships: Britain, Northern Ireland and Ireland 1965–1985

NORTHERN IRELAND IN THE 1960S AND ITS RELATIONS WITH THE REPUBLIC OF IRELAND

INTRODUCTION: THE EMERGENCE AND DEVELOPMENT OF NORTHERN IRELAND 1920–63

Northern Ireland was established by the 1920 Government of Ireland Act. This Act partitioned Ireland into two parts:

- a 26-county Southern Ireland (which later became the Irish Free State)
- a six-county Northern Ireland.

The population of Northern Ireland reacted to the new arrangements differently:

- **Unionists** – who were mostly Protestants – were delighted. The new state had a substantial Protestant majority guaranteeing their control of the government.
- **Nationalists** – most of whom were Catholics – were deeply upset; they wanted to be part of the rest of Ireland, governed by a parliament in Dublin.

WHAT YOU NEED TO KNOW

This topic is background information and will not be asked about directly on the exam. However, you should be aware of these facts, particularly those that help explain the problems that emerged in Northern Ireland in the 1960s.

VIOLENCE AND DISCRIMINATION

As a result, most Unionists felt that Nationalists could not be trusted and in this atmosphere of distrust the number of **sectarian** killings rocketed. The new government passed the Special Powers Act (1922), allowing it to arrest and detain suspects without trial. Other political responses to the seeming threat of Nationalism included:

- The abolition of Proportional Representation (PR) for local elections. This meant that fewer Nationalists would be elected to councils.
- The redrawing of the boundaries of local council areas to ensure Unionist control even where there was a nationalist majority. This was known as **gerrymandering** and the most infamous example of the practice was in the city of Derry/Londonderry.
- Allowing only those who paid **rates** to vote in local elections. For every £10 paid in rates one vote was given, up to a maximum of seven. This usually resulted in extra votes for the wealthy – who tended to be Protestant; and no votes for the poor – who were mostly – but not wholly – Catholic.

Discrimination was also practised against Catholics in other ways:

- Catholics were given fewer houses than Protestants by the Unionist-controlled councils as ownership of a house gave a vote in local elections.
- The quality of much Catholic housing was inferior.
- Catholics were less likely to have a job than Protestants.

DEVELOPMENTS UP TO 1963

By and large this situation remained unchanged until the 1960s, although in the late 1940s the Welfare State was introduced to improve living conditions.

However, relations with the South (the Republic of Ireland since 1949) remained tense, particularly as Articles II and III of its 1937 constitution laid claim to the whole of the island. Furthermore, an IRA campaign in opposition to the border between 1956–62 reinforced the Unionist government's view that Nationalists were untrustworthy. This was despite the fact that the campaign failed due to a lack of Nationalist support.

A NEW PREMIER

WHAT YOU NEED TO KNOW

You must be able to explain **why** O'Neill wanted to improve the economy, **how** he tried to do this and **what** the results of his policies were.

In March 1963 Captain Terence O'Neill became Prime Minister of Northern Ireland. O'Neill was born on 10 September 1914 to an aristocratic family. Following school he worked for a time in the City of London. During World War II he served in the Irish Guards. In 1946 he was elected MP for the Bannside constituency in the Stormont Parliament. Over the next 17 years he held a number of government positions including Parliamentary Secretary to the Ministry of Health and Local Government, Minister of Home Affairs, Minister of Education and Minister of Finance. Right from the start, O'Neill's leadership was undermined as most of the Unionist Party's (OUP) MPs had wanted another minister, Brian Faulkner, to get the job. However, at that time the OUP leader was decided by a group of senior party members, not by election.

IMPROVING THE ECONOMY

O'Neill's main concern lay with improving the economy. To this end the following measures were either proposed or introduced:

- £900 million of investment and the creation of five economic zones to update existing industries and attract new ones
- modernisation of the road and railway network (including closing seemingly unprofitable railway lines)
- co-operation with the Dublin-based Irish Trades Union Congress, whose support was important for economic development
- the establishment of an Economic Council under Brian Faulkner to drive forward the modernisation of the economy
- the creation of a Ministry of Development to drive economic revival
- the establishment of a new city called Craigavon
- the development of a new university in Coleraine to help develop a skilled workforce.

SUCCESS AND FAILURE

These policies were soon having a positive impact:

- Multinational firms such as Michelin, DuPont, Goodyear, ICI and Grundig took advantage of generous investment grants and tax allowances to open factories in Northern Ireland.
- The construction of a motorway system was begun.
- An oil refinery was opened in Belfast.
- A new airport was under development.
- Links with the Republic of Ireland resulted in the signing of an agreement on the supply of electricity from the south.

In total over 35,000 new jobs were created during the 1960s, but at the same time over 20,000 were lost in the ailing traditional industries such as linen manufacture.

This was not the only bad economic news:

- Between 1963 and 1969 the government had to give money to shipbuilders Harland & Wolff to keep it afloat.
- Unemployment averaged between 7 and 8 per cent.
- Several companies refused grants to open factories west of the River Bann, seeing the area as too remote from their export markets.

ACTIVITIES

1. Create a spider diagram illustrating the economic measures introduced by O'Neill's government.
2. Analyse O'Neill's economic policies using the headings (i) Successes and (ii) Failures.

This last fact alone had significant implications, not only for unemployment in the west (over 12.5 per cent) but also for feeding allegations of bias in government policy. This was because the majority of the population in the west was Nationalist.

O'NEILL'S POLITICAL POLICIES

WHAT YOU NEED TO KNOW

It is essential that you are able to explain **why** O'Neill wanted to improve relations with the Republic and within Northern Ireland and **what steps** he took to achieve this.

O'Neill realised that economic reform alone would not change Northern Ireland. There would also have to be social and political modernisation – to end discrimination and to help enable Nationalists to identify more strongly with the state – and improvements in relations with the Republic of Ireland – to benefit the economy. As someone with both Gaelic and **planter** ancestry, O'Neill believed that he was the right man for the job.

THE HAND OF FRIENDSHIP: DUBLIN

On 14 January 1965 the first face-to-face meeting of Ireland's main leaders since 1925 took place at Stormont when O'Neill met with the *Taoiseach* Seán Lemass. O'Neill defended the meeting by arguing that both systems shared 'the same rivers, the same mountains and some of the same problems'. In 1967 O'Neill met with Lemass' successor, Jack Lynch.

THE HAND OF FRIENDSHIP: NORTHERN NATIONALISTS

Within Northern Ireland O'Neill tried to improve relations with the Nationalist community by:

- visiting Cardinal William Conway, Archbishop of Armagh and spiritual leader of Ireland's Catholics
- offering official condolences on the death of Pope John XXIII in June 1963
- visiting Catholic schools and hospitals
- increasing the financial support provided for Catholic schools and hospitals (such as Belfast's Mater Infirmorum Hospital).

ACTIVITY

Create a spider diagram illustrating the steps taken by O'Neill to improve relations with Dublin and Northern Ireland's Nationalists.

REACTIONS TO O'NEILL'S POLICIES, 1963–7

WHAT YOU NEED TO KNOW

It is essential that you are able to explain **who** supported O'Neill, **who** opposed him and **why** this was the case.

UNIONIST REACTIONS

There was both support and opposition within the Unionist community for O'Neill's attempts to change Northern Ireland.

O'Neill's support among ordinary members of the OUP had never been total. Indeed, O'Neill did not even inform his own cabinet colleagues of Seán Lemass' January 1965 visit before it happened.

Evidence of the divisions within the OUP over the visit was clear when Brian Faulkner condemned O'Neill's failure to consult his cabinet. This suggests that the idea for the visit was O'Neill's alone.

That said, when Lemass' successor as *Taoiseach*, Jack Lynch, visited Northern Ireland in December 1967, the visit was agreed in cabinet, implying that by then such a visit had become more acceptable.

THE EMERGENCE OF REVEREND IAN PAISLEY

While there was no widespread hostile public reaction to the Lemass visit, there was strong objection from the **Moderator** of the Free Presbyterian Church, Reverend Ian Paisley. In addition to his concerns about the influence of the Catholic Church in the Republic, Paisley objected to any links with the South, especially as Articles II and III of its constitution laid claim to the whole island of Ireland. When Lynch visited in 1967, Paisley illustrated his continuing opposition by snowballing the *Taoiseach's* car. On the same day, Paisley and his supporters also carried placards describing O'Neill as a '**Lundy**'.

Throughout the rest of the decade Paisley's support grew as many Unionists came to fear the implications of O'Neill's new policies and to resent the failure of such policies to improve their own lives. In the short term, however, O'Neill was delighted with the success the OUP enjoyed in the November 1965 general election when it won 38 out of 52 seats. This seemed to suggest satisfaction with his policies.

VIOLENCE AND DIVISION

Tensions increased in 1966 with the commemorations for the 50th anniversaries of the Easter Rising and the Battle of the Somme. Rioting broke out. Then two Catholics died in May and June 1966, the result of a series of gun attacks by the re-emerging **UVF**. O'Neill responded by banning the organisation.

As the situation worsened, O'Neill found that his limited support within his own party was weakening. In September 1966 he revealed a plot by OUP **backbenchers** to remove him as leader. There were also growing rumours of opposition from Deputy Prime Minister, Brian Faulkner and Agriculture Minister, Harry West.

NATIONALIST REACTIONS: SATISFACTION AND DISAPPOINTMENT

At first Catholic leaders, political and religious, reacted warmly to O'Neill's attempts to hold out the hand of friendship. The visit of Lemass to Stormont was followed by the decision of the Nationalist Party to take up the role of official opposition in Stormont for the first time in its history.

However, O'Neill's policies also raised expectations, some of which were unlikely to be met given the growing tensions within Unionism. This annoyance was particularly felt among a new generation of Catholics:

- There was outrage at the decision to name the new city linking Portadown and Lurgan, Craigavon, after Northern Ireland's first Prime Minister.
- There were accusations that O'Neill's economic policies favoured the Protestant east at the expense of the Catholic west:
  - With the exception of Derry/Londonderry, all the places earmarked for economic development were in Protestant areas.
  - Unemployment was higher west of the Bann.
  - Despite significant cross-community protest, a new university was sited in the mainly Protestant town of Coleraine rather than in the mainly nationalist Derry/Londonderry, Northern Ireland's second city.
- No significant attempts were made to increase Catholic membership of various health and education bodies.

ACTIVITIES

1. Analyse Unionist reactions to O'Neill's policies under the following headings:
   - Evidence of Unionist support
   - Evidence of opposition from within the OUP
   - Reverend Ian Paisley
   - UVF
2. Create a spider diagram illustrating the evidence put forward by Nationalists to suggest that O'Neill's reforms were biased against them.

NICRA: BACKGROUND

WHAT YOU NEED TO KNOW

You should know **all** of the key points about NICRA's origins, aims and tactics and about the different reactions to them.

ORIGINS

The Northern Ireland Civil Rights Association (NICRA) was established at the start of 1967. The group took much of its inspiration from the United States where Martin Luther King's campaign had employed non-violent methods of **civil disobedience** to achieve equal opportunities for blacks.

At the same time there were other sources of encouragement in the period following NICRA's establishment, notably the student demonstrations that took place in France during 1968.

NICRA'S AIMS

Set up as a non-sectarian movement, NICRA did not seek to end partition; rather it sought to:

- Achieve 'one man, one vote'. This would allow a vote to all people over the age of 18. It would also remove the multiple votes of business owners.
- Ensure the fair allocation of council houses. The possession of a vote in council elections depended upon being a ratepayer – basically a

householder. The fewer the number of Catholics who possessed a property, the fewer could vote.
- End gerrymandering – the practice of drawing electoral boundaries in a way that benefited one community over the other.
- Prevent discrimination in the allocation of government jobs of which there was widespread evidence.
- Remove the operation of the Special Powers Act which allowed the government to arrest and detain people without holding a trial.
- Disband the B Specials, the sole remnant of the three-pronged **Ulster Special Constabulary**, which had been established in September 1920 to help fight the IRA during the War of Independence.
- Establish a formal complaints procedure against local authorities to report breaches in the above areas.

SUPPORT AND REACTION

Support for NICRA came from across the community. In particular it came from:

- Catholics who had benefited from the introduction of free education in the late 1940s. They had seen the growing self-confidence of Catholics elsewhere in the world. They were also less than happy with the performance of Eddie McAteer's Nationalist Party. Its only policy seemed to be the ending of partition.
- Liberal Protestants who sympathised with some of NICRA's demands and who believed that making Northern Ireland fairer for all of its inhabitants would undermine demands for a United Ireland.
- Other groups including communists, academics and trade unionists.

At the same time there was much suspicion from within the Unionist population. Some felt that NICRA was simply intent on causing trouble and was nothing more than a front for the IRA, while others believed that it was only interested in Catholic rights – as opposed to the rights of all – and would undermine the position of Protestants and even the continued existence of Northern Ireland by pushing for a united Ireland.

ACTIVITIES

1. Analyse NICRA under the following headings:
   - Date of establishment
   - Sources of inspiration
   - Tactics
   - Position on border
2. Create a spider diagram indicating NICRA's aims.
3. Examine attitudes to NICRA and its campaign by explaining who supported it and why and who opposed it and why.

NICRA: EVENTS

WHAT YOU NEED TO KNOW

Examiners will expect you to be able to write about NICRA's early marches, their impact and the five-point reform programme.

MARCHING FOR HOUSES

NICRA's first march was held on 24 August 1968 between Coalisland and Dungannon. This followed the decision of Dungannon Council to give a council house in the village of Caledon to a nineteen-year-old Protestant woman. The event passed off without incident.

VIOLENCE IN DERRY/LONDONDERRY

In order to highlight what were seen as inequalities in Londonderry Corporation's housing policy, a march was organised for 5 October 1968. In response the **Apprentice Boys** organisation threatened to hold a rival march. The government responded by banning the holding of any march; however, NICRA rejected this ban.

Although the crowd that turned up on 5 October was relatively small, it was accompanied by an **RTE** camera crew. That night televised pictures beamed across the world showing the heavy-handed tactics used by the police to break up the rally.

Further NICRA marches – including one in Newry in January 1969 – made the situation even worse. Quite often violence resulted. There were several reasons for this:

- NICRA going ahead with banned marches
- marches were seen as provocative, especially when they went through Protestant areas
- NICRA marches coming into contact with Unionist counter-demonstrations.

THE FIVE-POINT REFORM PROGRAMME

As a result of the unrest a reform programme was announced on 22 November. It included five main proposals, all of which were to be in place by the end of 1971.

1 The allocation of council housing on a **points system**.
2 The replacement of Londonderry Corporation by a Development Commission.
3 The removal of parts of the 1922 Special Powers Act.
4 Local government reforms, including the ending of extra votes for business owners.
5 The appointment of an **ombudsman** to investigate complaints.

CALM BEFORE THE STORM?

In the short-term, protests and counter-protests continued and so, on 9 December, O'Neill appeared on television to stress the starkness of the situation. In particular he asked NICRA's leaders to help to restore calm. This became known as O'Neill's 'Ulster at the Crossroads' speech.

At first his message seemed to have the desired effect and NICRA protests were called off. However, there were additional problems to deal with:

- The reforms had caused dismay among those Unionists who opposed concessions to the threat of violence and who now felt that their position was under threat.
- O'Neill faced further opposition from within his own party, with Home Affairs Minister William Craig condemning his television speech and arguing that he was acting under pressure from the British government. Craig was sacked.

ACTIVITIES

1 Examine NICRA's Coalisland–Dungannon and Derry/Londonderry marches under the following headings:
   - Date
   - Reasons
   - Outcome
2 Create a spider diagram to explain why NICRA marches often ended in violence.
3 Create a spider diagram illustrating O'Neill's Five-Point Reform Programme.
4 Analyse O'Neill's television appearance and its aftermath under the following headings:
   - Background
   - Impact
   - Unionism divided

A MORE RADICAL MOVEMENT EMERGES

WHAT YOU NEED TO KNOW

There were a lot of reasons for O'Neill's resignation in 1969. You must be able to identify the different factors, explain them and comment on their impact.

PEOPLE'S DEMOCRACY

Although NICRA stopped marching, its decision was ignored by the recently formed People's Democracy. This group, made up mainly of university students, had emerged out of anger at the violence NICRA had faced in October 1968 and their desire to cause disruption to the Stormont administration. It had developed broadly similar demands:

- one man, one vote
- fair boundaries
- houses on need
- jobs on merit
- free speech
- repeal of the Special Powers Act.

Unhappy with the limited nature of O'Neill's Five-Point Reform Programme, People's Democracy announced that it was holding a march between Belfast and Derry/Londonderry, from 1–4 January 1969.

AMBUSH AT BURNTOLLET

Much of the march was to go through Protestant areas, forcing the police to enforce different routes to avoid confrontation. However, on the third day the marchers were the target of a violent ambush at Burntollet Bridge, an attack that the police seemed to do little to deflect. Later on the same night, tensions were further raised in Derry/Londonderry when police rampaged through Nationalist areas of the city.

REACTIONS TO BURNTOLLET

NICRA now started to march again. The first march was held in Newry and again violence resulted. In response O'Neill established the Cameron Commission to investigate the increasing violence. This led two cabinet members (including Brian Faulkner) to resign. Faulkner argued that O'Neill was too weak to control the situation.

Faulkner's opinion of O'Neill seemed to be gaining support within the OUP with 12 MPs calling for his resignation on 30 January 1969. Instead O'Neill called a general election – which he termed the 'Crossroads Election' – in an attempt to prove that he had public support.

THE 'CROSSROADS ELECTION'

The election took place on 24 February 1969; however, the result was not what O'Neill had wanted:

- There was a reduction in Unionist support and divisions of loyalty among the OUP MPs elected.
- There was little or no evidence of the hoped-for support from Catholic voters.
- O'Neill, who had never before had to face a challenger in his own constituency, polled only 1,400 votes more than his opponent, Reverend Ian Paisley.

O'Neill struggled on for another two months, but with his party now hopelessly divided and with a further deterioration in the political situation caused by increasing violence and confrontation, he resigned on 28 April 1969.

A NEW LEADER

O'Neill was succeeded by his cousin, Major James Chichester Clark. He had resigned from the government less than a week earlier in protest at O'Neill's decision to introduce one man, one vote in time for the next council elections. Then Chichester Clark had argued that the timing of the measure was wrong; now he declared he would continue with O'Neill's reform programme.

ACTIVITIES

1. Create a spider diagram indicating People's Democracy's aims.
2. Analyse the People's Democracy march using the following headings:
   - Reasons
   - Events
   - Results
3. Examine the 1969 'Crossroads Election' using the following headings:
   - Why was it called the 'Crossroads Election'?
   - What were the results?
4. Analyse O'Neill's resignation under the following headings:
   - Date
   - Reasons
   - Successor

ESCALATION OF POLITICAL AND CIVIL UNREST

THE SUMMER OF 1969

Post-Burntollet civil rights protests were more confrontational than ever and were followed by serious rioting in Belfast. As the July–August marching season approached, grave concerns were raised over the likely impact on an already tense situation:

- The Stormont government was worried whether the already stretched security forces would be able to cope with a further increase in violence.
- The London government had become concerned enough to establish a cabinet committee on Northern Ireland.
- The Dublin government, anxious about the safety of the Catholic minority community, sent an intelligence officer to the North to watch what was happening.

To make matters worse, armed groups seemed to be emerging:

- among Loyalists, angry at what they saw as concessions to Nationalists
- among Republicans, apprehensive at their inability to protect Nationalists.

WHAT YOU NEED TO KNOW

From mid-1969 onwards the political situation really began to deteriorate. One of the first political responses was the Downing Street Declaration and associated reforms. Make sure that you know the **key terms** and **reactions**.

A LONG HOT SUMMER

Sectarian violence broke out in Belfast in July where the violence mainly took the form of house burning, mostly by Loyalists, resulting in many having to leave their homes in areas such as Bombay Street. Seven people lost their lives during this period, while 100 were wounded. In Derry/Londonderry rioting began following the annual Apprentice Boys parade on 12 August. In total the rioting during what became known as the Battle of the Bogside lasted for 50 hours. Finally calm was restored by using a small number of British troops, as requested by Nationalist politicians, among others. However, violence continued elsewhere.

In the middle of this violence, *Taoiseach* Jack Lynch issued a statement outlining his concerns at the deteriorating situation. This statement, and the accompanying movement of Irish troops and field hospitals to the border, did little to ease tension.

THE DOWNING STREET DECLARATION

On 19 August Chichester Clark met the British Prime Minister, Harold Wilson. The outcome was the Downing Street Declaration. This declaration aimed to reassure both communities:

- Nationalists were told that 'every citizen of Northern Ireland is entitled to the same equality of treatment and freedom from discrimination as [exists] in the rest of the UK irrespective of political views or religion'.
- Unionists were told that 'Northern Ireland should not cease to be part of the UK without the consent of the people of Northern Ireland'.

ADDITIONAL REFORMS

Further reforms were announced or introduced in the following weeks:

- The introduction of 'one man, one vote', and an end to gerrymandering.
- A committee on policing chaired by Lord Hunt.
- A **tribunal** to investigate recent disturbances, led by Lord Scarman.
- A single housing authority took over housing functions from local councils.
- Measures to prevent discrimination in public employment.
- The creation of a Ministry of Community Relations.

There were also moves to improve the economy:

- a £2 million programme of job-creating schemes
- increases in investment grants.

UNIONIST REACTIONS

Despite the reassurances of the Downing Street Declaration, many Unionists were concerned at what they saw as continuing concessions to Nationalists. The final straw came when the Hunt Report was published. It recommended:

- disarming the RUC
- disbanding the B Specials and replacing them with the Ulster Defence Regiment (UDR), a part-time force under army control.

Angered at the proposals, violence erupted on Belfast's Shankill Road.

NATIONALIST REACTIONS

Nationalists reacted positively to the reforms, believing that a positive future involving a reformed political system was now within their grasp.

ACTIVITIES

1. Examine the violence of the summer of 1969 using the following headings:
   - Location of violence
   - Details
2. Analyse the Downing Street Declaration using the headings:
   - Points to reassure Unionists
   - Points to reassure Nationalists
3. Create a spider diagram identifying the various reforms that followed on from the Downing Street Declaration.
4. Make notes under the following headings:
   - Unionist reactions to reforms
   - Nationalist reactions to reforms

MILITARY AND PARAMILITARIES

WHAT YOU NEED TO KNOW

The split within the IRA, changing Nationalist attitudes to the British army and the growth of Protestant paramilitary groups are all key developments in 1969–70. You need to be able to explain the details behind all of these changes and their political implications.

PARAMILITARY SPLITS

In the last days of 1969 the IRA split into two parts:

- The Official IRA (OIRA), which continued to focus on establishing a **Marxist** Ireland. At the same time violence was still used until a ceasefire was called in May 1972. In 1974 the movement split again

with the emergence of the Irish Republican Socialist Party (IRSP) and the militant Irish Nationalist Liberation Army (INLA).
- The Provisional IRA (IRA), which claimed for itself the traditional role of defender of the Nationalist community.

By Easter 1970 the Provisional IRA had declared its objectives, which were:

- civil rights
- defence of the Catholic population
- the destruction of the Stormont government
- the removal of 'British **imperialism**' from Ireland.

THE IRA AND THE BRITISH ARMY

The IRA's campaign began to take off in earnest in the middle of 1970. This development placed the British army in a difficult position. Upon its arrival on the streets of Northern Ireland, the army had been welcomed by large sections of the Nationalist community as its protector from what was perceived to be a police force in which they felt unable to place any trust. Their arrival was also considered to be a rejection by the British government of the security policy followed by the Stormont administration. The army now felt, however, that it had no choice but to respond to the growing IRA threat and in doing so, it damaged the good relations built up with the Nationalist community. One example of this came in July 1970 when the Army imposed a 36-hour curfew on the Lower Falls area of Belfast while a house-to-house search for weapons was carried out. Although a number of weapons – as well as ammunition and explosives – were discovered, politically the search was a disaster. It undermined the army's previously good relationship with the Nationalist community and helped increase IRA membership.

PROTESTANT PARAMILITARIES

The Protestant paramilitaries also wanted to see an end to the current Stormont regime. They sought a return to the old days of Unionist domination. The UVF had grown and prospered against the background of NICRA's campaign and what was seen as O'Neill's appeasement of Catholics.

September 1971 saw the formation of the Ulster Defence Association (UDA). The UDA viewed itself as a defensive grouping that would resist Republican aggression. With over 30,000 members within a year, the government decided it was too large to ban.

FAULKNER REPLACES CHICHESTER CLARK

The levels of violence and destruction shot up during the remaining months of 1970 and into 1971. The Stormont government demanded a stronger response from Britain's new Conservative government; however, little happened, as London didn't want to alienate Nationalists even more. In despair at London's inaction, Chichester Clark resigned as Prime Minister on 20 March, to be replaced by Brian Faulkner.

ACTIVITIES

1. Explain the IRA split by writing a sentence under each of the following:
   - Focus of OIRA
   - OIRA use of violence
   - Split in OIRA
   - Focus of IRA
   - Aims of IRA
2. Explain the change in Nationalist attitudes to the British army under the following headings:
   - Initial attitude
   - Changed attitude
   - Reasons for change
   - Impact on IRA
3. Analyse the change within Unionist leadership in 1971 under the following headings:
   - Old Prime Minister
   - New Prime Minister
   - Reasons for the change

INTERNMENT AND BLOODY SUNDAY

WHAT YOU NEED TO KNOW

You need to be able to explain **why** internment was introduced, **why** it backfired and **how** it then linked in with events that culminated in Bloody Sunday.

INTERNMENT

In the summer of 1971 Northern Ireland Prime Minister Brian Faulkner persuaded the British government to allow him to re-introduce internment. It was introduced in response to growing unionist concerns about the Stormont government's failure to deal with escalating levels of violence, increased bombings and the threat to Northern Ireland's economy. Above all, Unionists argued that internment had worked well when previously used (in the 1920s, 1940s and 1950s) and thus should work well again. The British government was far from convinced that internment (introduced through Operation Demetrius on 9 August 1971) would work, but seemingly feared a Unionist backlash if they did not agree to its introduction.

Internment failed spectacularly as the intelligence was entirely out of date. Not one of the 452 men arrested was a leading member of the Provisional IRA. Those really sought, Faulkner himself later admitted, had 'escaped the net'. Moreover, despite the high levels of Loyalist violence, all those interned were Nationalists or civil rights supporters. The first Loyalists were not interned until February 1973.

REACTIONS TO INTERNMENT

There were a number of responses to internment:

- At first Unionists were happy; they believed internment had worked in the past and saw it as essential in ending IRA violence. However, their support decreased when the policy failed to reduce levels of violence, particularly against Protestant businesses. They also believed that internees could help with the location of IRA weapons, something that Faulkner believed did happen.
- Nationalists saw internment as one-sided in its application and open to substantial abuse. As a result, IRA membership increased. In addition, as the British army was involved in the implementation of internment, its increasingly poor relations with the Nationalist community deteriorated even further.

Increased violence and destruction followed the introduction of internment, leaving many dead and thousands homeless. From then until the end of the year, 143 people lost their lives violently. This was nearly five times as many as died in the first eight months of 1971. Increasing Republican violence resulted in the establishment of the paramilitary UDA in September 1971.

Along with other Nationalist and Republican Labour representatives, the **Social Democratic and Labour Party (SDLP)** called for people to withhold payment of rents and rates and for a withdrawal from local government and from Stormont. Civil rights marches were also organised, but the army's response also seemed to be hardening. A protest held at Magilligan Internment Camp on 22 January was met with baton charges and CS gas from the army.

BLOODY SUNDAY

In the aftermath of another anti-internment march in Derry/Londonderry eight days later, a riot developed. In response troops from the Parachute Regiment were ordered into the Bogside and shot 13 men dead. Thirteen more were injured, one of whom subsequently died of his wounds. An official inquiry headed by Lord Widgery failed to provide a satisfactory conclusion to the events of what became known as Bloody Sunday, although it did establish that none of those who died had been carrying a weapon when shot.

The events of Bloody Sunday had a number of results:

- Continued support for the government from the Unionist community which, while regretting the deaths, saw the march as illegal and provocative. Some in the Unionist community believed that the IRA was involved in the organisation of the march and that some of those killed had been armed.
- Given the belief that all of the victims were innocent and the Parachute Regiment attack was unprovoked, Nationalist hostility to the state was increased. This was symbolised by rioting in Nationalist areas and by the burning down of the British Embassy in Dublin.
- Britain faced international condemnation for the role it was playing in Northern Ireland.
- IRA membership grew – particularly in Derry/Londonderry – and its bombing campaign intensified.

ACTIVITIES

1. Examine internment under the following headings:
   - Reasons for introduction
   - Details
   - Reasons for failure
2. Create a spider diagram illustrating various responses to/impact of internment.
3. Examine Bloody Sunday under the following headings:
   - Background
   - Details
   - British government reaction
4. Create a spider diagram illustrating the various responses to Bloody Sunday.

The resulting increase in IRA violence and the government's failure to end it led to the formation in February 1972 of Ulster Vanguard. Headed by William Craig, the former Stormont minister, Vanguard was described as a co-ordinating body for traditional Loyalist groups. One of its meetings attracted 70,000 people.

DIRECT RULE

WHAT YOU NEED TO KNOW

You will be expected to be able to explain **what** Direct Rule was and to identify the reasons **why** the British government took this decision and explain **how** the different sides reacted to it.

SUSPENSION OF STORMONT

Faulkner now demanded the power to re-arm the RUC and re-establish the B Specials. Conservative Prime Minister Edward Heath responded by demanding control of law and order and justice; however, Faulkner refused. On 22 March 1972, Heath informed the Stormont government of proposals for the:

- transfer of security control to Westminster
- holding of a referendum on the future of the border
- gradual removal of internment
- appointment of a **Secretary of State** for Northern Ireland
- holding of talks with other parties in Northern Ireland in an attempt to establish a 'community government'.

The entire Northern Ireland government resigned, unable to accept the loss of control over security policy. On 24 March, Heath responded by suspending Stormont for a year (later extended) and introducing **Direct Rule**. He had come to the conclusion that Northern Ireland could not continue to be governed as it had been. William Whitelaw was appointed as the first Secretary of State.

REACTIONS TO THE END OF STORMONT

Most Unionists were horrified at the end of power at Stormont. The last hours of the Parliament were played out before a crowd estimated at 100,000. This came in the midst of a series of massive protest strikes and shutdowns, organised by Ulster Vanguard. There was also an increase in support for loyalist paramilitaries and a spate of sectarian killings, particularly in Belfast. Meanwhile, support for the DUP and other strongly Unionist parties also increased in the aftermath of the introduction of Direct Rule.

The SDLP and the Dublin government welcomed the chance for a new beginning. The IRA, although it had achieved one of its aims, stated its opposition to Direct Rule and announced its determination to continue its struggle to achieve a united Ireland. NICRA stated that its campaign for civil rights would continue.

1972: THE BLACKEST YEAR

1972 turned out to be the worst year of **the 'Troubles'**, despite the introduction of internment, Direct Rule and a two-week IRA ceasefire. By the end of the year, 496 people had lost their lives in a series of appalling atrocities which included:

- 21 July when the IRA detonated 20 bombs around Belfast. Nine civilians died on a day that became known as Bloody Friday.
- 31 July when, without warning, three IRA bombs exploded in the village of Claudy in Co. Derry/Londonderry. In total nine civilians lost their lives.

The British government responded on 31 July with Operation Motorman. This aimed to allow the army and police to reclaim control of the paramilitary-controlled **no-go areas** established in Belfast, Derry/Londonderry and elsewhere in 1969.

ACTIVITIES

1. Examine the reasons for the introduction of Direct Rule using the following headings:
   - Faulkner's demands
   - Heath's response
   - Heath's demands
   - Faulkner's response
   - Changes Heath proposed
   - Stormont government response
2. Create a spider diagram indicating the different reactions to the suspension of Stormont and the introduction of Direct Rule.
3. List the reasons why 1972 is known as the worst year of the 'Troubles'.

THE SEARCH FOR A SOLUTION

POWER SHARING

WHAT YOU NEED TO KNOW

You need to be able to explain **what** power-sharing was and **how** reactions to it undermined its chances of success. Equally important is your ability to explain **what** was agreed at Sunningdale and **why** the agreement was fatally flawed.

A NEW POLITICAL SYSTEM

On 20 March 1973, the British government published its proposals for the future of Northern Ireland.

The plans proposed a new assembly (parliament) elected by proportional representation. There would also be an executive (government). However, it was not to be given control over security or justice. In addition, the British government insisted that there would have to be:

- the sharing of power between Catholics and Protestants
- the formal recognition of an '**Irish Dimension**' through the creation of a Council of Ireland. This would allow for the discussion of common interests.

EARLY PROBLEMS

While Nationalists were broadly supportive, Unionism was divided in its reaction to the plans. Some of the OUP remained loyal to Brian Faulkner who was supporting the plans. Other Unionists – the remainder of the OUP, the **Democratic Unionist Party (DUP)** and the new Vanguard Unionist Progressive Party (set up by William Craig to oppose power-sharing) – joined together to form the **United Ulster Unionist Council (UUUC)** to oppose the plans. Apart from their opposition to any 'Irish Dimension', they saw the proposals as undemocratic and believed that power should not be shared with those who were not loyal to the Union.

The extent of these splits became clear when the results of the Assembly elections were announced in June. They revealed that the number of anti power-sharing Unionists elected was greater than the number of Unionists elected who supported power-sharing.

Party	Pro- or anti-power sharing	Percentage of vote	Number of seats won
Faulkner Unionists	Pro	29.3	24
UUUC Unionists	Anti	32.1	26
SDLP	Pro	22.1	19
APNI	Pro	9.2	8
Northern Ireland Labour Party (NILP)	Pro	2.6	1

AN EXECUTIVE IS FORMED

On 21 November, Whitelaw revealed the membership of the Power-Sharing Executive. Six ministries were to be held by Unionists, four by the SDLP and one by the **Alliance Party (APNI)**. There would also be four non-voting members of the Executive: two SDLP, one Unionist and one Alliance. The OUP's Brian Faulkner would head the executive while the SDLP's Gerry Fitt would be his deputy.

SUNNINGDALE

The discussions about the Council of Ireland took place at Sunningdale in Berkshire. The meeting brought together the leading politicians from Britain, Ireland and Northern Ireland. At one stage Reverend Ian Paisley and William Craig were asked to attend to give their views. Unsurprisingly they refused.

Agreement between the parties was finally reached in December 1973.

ACTIVITY

1 Analyse the March 1973 British government proposals for running Northern Ireland by writing a sentence about each of the following:
- Key elements of the proposals
- Nationalist response to the proposals
- Unionist response to the proposals (including the election results)
- Membership of the executive

The Sunningdale Agreement contained the following elements:

- London agreed not to oppose Irish unification if a majority of the Northern Ireland population desired it.
- Dublin accepted that Irish unity could only ever be achieved peacefully and with the consent of the majority of the people of Northern Ireland.
- A Council of Ministers with 14 members was to be established to help with the development of North–South co-operation. It would eventually be given decision-making powers.
- A 60-member Consultative Assembly would be elected by the Dáil and the Assembly at some future date.
- Also at some future date control over internal security issues would be returned to the Stormont Assembly.
- Approval of the decisions made at Sunningdale was to take place at a future conference.

ACTIVITIES

2 Create a spider diagram showing the key points of the Sunningdale Agreement.

3 Analyse the Sunningdale Agreement using the headings:
- Unionist understanding
- Nationalist understanding
- Republican reaction
- Loyalist reaction

PROBLEMS FOR THE FUTURE

On the surface the agreement looked promising; the problem was that both sides believed that they had agreed to something entirely different:

- The SDLP saw the agreement as paving the way towards the creation of closer ties between North and South.
- Faulkner saw it as a mere token, which he had agreed to as a way to get Dublin to accept the position of Northern Ireland as part of the UK.

Republicans were also lukewarm in their support, seeing the new system as proposing substantially less than what they sought.

In the shorter term, however, Faulkner faced more serious problems. On 10 December Loyalist paramilitaries announced the formation of an Ulster Army Council to resist any significant 'Irish Dimension'. Nor did the IRA seem any more satisfied, setting off a series of bombs in London in the week before Christmas.

THE EXECUTIVE IN OPERATION

WHAT YOU NEED TO KNOW

The chances of success for power-sharing – already slim – were further undermined by the 1974 Westminster general election and by the UWC strike. Make sure that you can explain these important developments fully.

The Power-Sharing Executive took up office on 1 January 1974. Almost immediately its future was plunged into doubt by events within the OUP:

- A meeting of the OUP's ruling body, the Ulster Unionist Council, on 4 January voted to reject Sunningdale. Faulkner immediately resigned as party leader and was replaced by Harry West. However, Faulkner retained the support of 19 of the 21 OUP Assembly members and so was able to remain at the head of the Power-Sharing Executive.
- On 28 February a Westminster general election took place. With 80 per cent of the vote, 11 of the 12 Northern Ireland constituencies were won by the UUUC.

The election also resulted in a change in government in London, with Labour returning to power under Harold Wilson.

STRIKE

On 14 May 1974 a general strike began in Northern Ireland. It was organised by the Ulster Workers' Council (UWC), a group of Protestant trade unionists who had gained substantial amounts political and paramilitary support.

Initially support for the strike was limited but UDA intimidation and improved co-ordination by the UWC ensured that by the end of the week much of Northern Ireland had come to a standstill. Attempts by some of Northern Ireland's trade unions to organise a back-to-work demonstration on 21 May met with little support – only 200 turned up.

Tensions were further heightened on 17 May when car bombs exploded in Dublin and Monaghan. It was believed that Loyalists were behind the attacks which claimed 27 lives (five more of the injured later died of their wounds).

ACTIVITY

1 Analyse the initial problems facing the Power-Sharing Executive by writing a brief explanation of the following headings:
- Faulkner's problems with the OUP
- Faulkner's position as Chief Executive
- February 1974 general election

Wilson's Intervention

Although there were by now 17,500 soldiers in the province, the army was hesitant about taking on the strikers, arguing that the strike was political and not a terrorist action. The British Prime Minister, however, was losing patience with the situation and appeared on television on 25 May to denounce the strike and call its organisers 'spongers'. This speech infuriated Unionists and more than anything else, ensured that the strike continued.

When the government ordered the army to take over fuel supplies the UWC ordered a total shutdown across Northern Ireland. Seeing no obvious solution and with the British and SDLP still refusing to negotiate with the UWC, Faulkner resigned as Chief Executive on 28 May. The other Unionist members of the executive resigned with him, thus ending power sharing.

Having achieved its goal, the UWC ended the strike on 29 May. The Assembly was suspended on 30 May and, after five months' absence, direct rule was reintroduced.

It is impossible to know if power-sharing could have worked if it had been given more time to establish firm roots. It seems clear that many of those involved in the power-sharing initiative were not as fully committed to its success as was needed. This lack of commitment – coupled with intense opposition from some quarters – was enough to ensure the failure of this attempted solution, and the continuation of political unrest.

ACTIVITY

2 Analyse the UWC strike by explaining the following headings:
- Reasons for calling the strike
- Initial support
- How support increased
- Strike impact
- Bombs in the Republic
- Wilson's speech
- Army involvement
- Ministerial resignations

DEVELOPMENTS 1975–80

WHAT YOU NEED TO KNOW

The key development in this section is the removal of Special Category Status and, most importantly, the IRA's reaction to it.

NEW SECURITY POLICIES

Following the collapse of the Power-Sharing Executive, the British government pursued policies of:

- Ulsterisation – reducing the strength of the army in Northern Ireland while increasing the size of the RUC and UDR.
- Criminalisation – the end of **Special Category Status** for those convicted of terrorist offences. This meant that those convicted after March 1976 would be treated in the same way as other criminals. They would be housed in a new prison consisting of H-shaped blocks, which had been built at the Maze outside Belfast.

Although the numbers of deaths as a result of violence began to decrease in the latter years of the 1970s, there were still some appalling incidents such as the IRA firebombing of the La Mon House Hotel outside Belfast, resulting in the deaths of 12 people.

As a second decade of violence dawned, however, violence seemed to be on the increase again and a solution to the violence seemed as far away as ever, despite the election, in April 1979, of a new Conservative government led by Margaret Thatcher.

THE 1980 HUNGER STRIKE

IRA prisoners – who saw themselves as soldiers fighting for Ireland's freedom – detested the policy of criminalisation. Their initial reaction was to refuse to wear prison clothes, instead covering themselves with blankets. This blanket protest was followed in 1978 by the dirty protest, when prisoners smeared their cell walls with excrement rather than having to slop out. By late 1980 over 340 of the 837 Republican prisoners were involved in the protest.

Public demonstrations in support of the protests met with little success. Even attacks on prison warders proved ineffective. Therefore in late 1980 the IRA began a group hunger strike as a last method of achieving their demands. This historically-successful tactic was called off in December, however, without anything having been achieved, although the prisoners believed that a deal had been reached on the wearing of their own clothes.

ACTIVITIES

1 Write a definition of:
- Ulsterisation
- Criminalisation
- Special Category Status

2 Analyse the IRA response to criminalisation by explaining the following terms:
- Blanket protest
- Dirty protest
- 1980 hunger strike

THE 1981 HUNGER STRIKE

BOBBY SANDS

On 1 March 1981 a second hunger strike began, led by Bobby Sands, the IRA prisoners' Officer Commanding. This time prisoners joined the protest at intervals, making the strike last longer and maximising its impact.

Although the hunger strike gained huge publicity and the sympathy of many in the Nationalist community, it did not change government policy. Therefore when Frank Maguire, the Independent MP for Fermanagh–South Tyrone died, Republicans saw their chance to increase pressure on the British and put Sands up as a candidate. On the fortieth day of his strike, Sands, standing as an Anti-H Block candidate, was elected to Westminster.

Despite huge amounts of international pressure on both sides, neither would compromise and on 5 May Sands died. His funeral was attended by an estimated 100,000 mourners. The strike continued until 3 October 1981, by which time nine other prisoners had died. In the same period 61 people died as a result of the violence that erupted in reaction to the hunger strikers' deaths.

CONCESSIONS GRANTED

No concessions were made during the hunger strike. However, within a week of its end a number of concessions were announced. These included:

- Prisoners would be allowed to wear their own clothes.
- The 50 per cent reduction in length of sentence lost by those involved in protests would be restored.
- A greater number of prison visits would be permitted.
- A greater degree of association among prisoners would be permitted.

These concessions resulted in the protests in favour of special category status all but ending by late October 1981.

AFTERMATH

In the aftermath of the hunger strikes new problems were emerging for the British government:

- Increased Nationalist alienation from the state, resulting from what was seen as Prime Minister Margaret Thatcher's heavy-handed approach to the hunger strikers, whose demands were viewed as reasonable.
- The growth in support for the Republican movement.
- Unionists, while glad that the government had not given into the demands of the hunger strikers, who they saw as murderers and criminals, were increasingly voicing their anxieties at the growth in support for the IRA (as demonstrated by the huge numbers attending the funerals of Bobby Sands and other hunger-strikers) and the seeming weaknesses of the province's security provisions which allowed IRA violence to continue.
- The Irish government was pushing for the introduction of a new political initiative to end the 'Troubles'.

THE RISE OF SINN FÉIN

Sands' victory in Fermanagh–South Tyrone showed Republicans that there was much to gain from involvement in the political process at a time when the British government was enjoying increasing success in its undercover campaign against Republicans. That his victory had not been a fluke was proved when his election agent, Owen Carron, won the seat at the by-election following Sands' death.

The official adoption of a policy of increasing involvement in politics came at the 1981 Sinn Féin ***Ard Fheis***. Here, the delegates approved the movement's plan of contesting elections while also continuing to use

WHAT YOU NEED TO KNOW

The 1981 hunger strike is another turning point. You must be able to explain **why** it took place, **what** happened and **how** it impacted on Northern Ireland politics.

ACTIVITIES

1. Examine the 1981 hunger strike by making a note of the following:
   - Leader of 1981 hunger strike
   - Constituency in which May 1981 by-election took place
   - Date hunger strike ended
   - Number of prisoners who died
   - Number of people who died in related violence
   - Number of concessions made during hunger strike
2. Create a spider diagram illustrating the concessions made after the hunger strike ended.

extra-constitutional methods to achieve its aims. This became known as the 'Armalite and Ballot Box' strategy.

The results of following elections clearly revealed the growth in support for Sinn Féin among Nationalist voters. The party was soon winning an increasing number of local council seats. Then, in the June 1983 Westminster general election, the party's President, Gerry Adams, defeated Gerry Fitt for the West Belfast seat. The British Government was growing increasingly concerned that Sinn Féin might even replace the SDLP as the main Nationalist party in the province. This prospect also worried the SDLP. The party, led since 1979 by John Hume, was looking more and more to Dublin for support.

Now with both governments co-operating ever more closely in the face of Sinn Féin's growth, there was the possibility that the SDLP might again have a significant input into the future direction of the province.

At the same time the levels of violence – while lower than the 1970s – still gave considerable cause for concern. On 6 December 1982, 17 people, 11 of whom were soldiers, died when an INLA bomb exploded in Ballykelly. The INLA had emerged in 1974 from a split in the Official IRA.

ACTIVITY

3 Create a spider diagram explaining the different reactions to/impact of the hunger strike.

THE ANGLO–IRISH AGREEMENT

Faced with continuing violence and increasing support for Sinn Féin, the British and Irish governments decided to work more closely together. The outcome was the Anglo–Irish Agreement.

The Anglo–Irish Agreement was signed by Thatcher and *Taoiseach* Garrett FitzGerald on 15 November 1985. Historians have provided different reasons as to why it was signed:

- Thatcher realised that unless she dealt with Nationalist alienation in Northern Ireland, she would not be able to improve the security situation. The IRA's attempt to kill her at the 1984 Conservative Party Conference in Brighton brought the problem particularly into focus.
- The Irish Government's previous attempted solution, the **New Ireland Forum** (1983-1984) had failed due to a lack of Unionist engagement, the exclusion of Republicans from its discussions and Thatcher's outright rejection of all of its suggested solutions.
- FitzGerald hoped that reduced Nationalist alienation and reform of the security forces in Northern Ireland would undermine the minority's toleration of the IRA and support for Sinn Féin.

WHAT YOU NEED TO KNOW

Three important areas for you to know here: **why** the agreement was signed, **what** it said and **how** different groups and individuals reacted to it.

WHAT WAS AGREED?

The key terms of the Agreement were:

- The establishment of an intergovernmental conference, headed by the Secretary of State and the Irish Foreign Minister. This would deal with security, legal and political issues and improving cross-border co-operation.
- A permanent **secretariat** made up of northern and southern civil servants would provide administrative support to the conference.
- **Devolution** would only occur if there was agreement on the sharing of power.

The Agreement clearly recognised that the Republic had a role to play in the government of Northern Ireland. At the same time Dublin accepted that a united Ireland was a long-term goal that would only happen with the agreement of a majority of Northern Ireland population.

REACTIONS

While the Agreement passed through both Westminster and the Dáil without any real problems, it met with a wide variety of reactions elsewhere.

Northern Ireland

Unionists

Unionists felt that they had been abandoned by their own government and believed that they were now in a process that would eventually result in a united Ireland. They were annoyed that they had been kept in the dark during the negotiations leading up to the Agreement. Only the Alliance Party did not condemn the Agreement outright.

Nationalists

The SDLP had been given more of a role in the creation of the Agreement than any other party in the North. It therefore saw the accord as an opportunity to create a better way of life for all those living in the province.

Republicans

Sinn Féin condemned the agreement, arguing that rather than bringing a united Ireland closer, it actually made the division of Ireland more permanent since Dublin was now recognising the existence of Northern Ireland and accepting that a united Ireland was a long-term aim that would only happen with the consent of a majority in Northern Ireland.

Republic of Ireland

The Fianna Fáil opposition party led by Charles Haughey condemned the Agreement due to the recognition being given by Dublin to Britain's right to be in Northern Ireland. A prominent Irish Labour Party Senator, Mary Robinson, resigned from her party because the Agreement was unacceptable to the Unionist community.

Britain

The Agreement enjoyed overwhelming cross-party support at Westminster but individual members of the British Parliament were not so happy. Ian Gow, the Prime Minister's former Parliamentary Private Secretary and now a Treasury Minister, resigned from his position in the government. He argued that the Agreement was won by violence and would make the situation in the province worse rather than better.

ACTIVITIES

1 Analyse the Anglo–Irish Agreement using the following headings:
- Reasons why it was signed
- Key terms
- Structures established

2 Explain the reactions to the Anglo–Irish Agreement by completing the following:
- Who supported it and why?
- Who opposed it and why?

CAMPAIGN OF OPPOSITION TO THE ANGLO–IRISH AGREEMENT

WHAT YOU NEED TO KNOW

Make sure that you can identify all of the different methods employed by Unionists to oppose the Anglo–Irish Agreement and can comment on whether or not they worked.

Unionist politicians decided that the best way of opposing the Anglo–Irish Agreement was by a campaign of non-cooperation with the British government. However, they were also keen to demonstrate the depth and breadth of Unionist opposition to what they termed the 'Dublin **Diktat**'.

The campaign against the Agreement took a variety of forms:

- Bonfires burning effigies of Margaret Thatcher, Irish Foreign Minister Peter Barry and other members of the Dublin government.
- Marches to the headquarters of the new Anglo–Irish Secretariat. On a number of occasions these ended in violence.
- A huge protest rally was held at Belfast's City Hall on 23 November 1985, attended by an estimated 100,000 people.
- All 15 Unionist MPs resigned their seats at Westminster but then stood for them again in the resulting by-elections. The aim was to show the strength of Unionist opposition through the total number of votes the candidates received.
- A Unionist 'Day of Action' was arranged for 3 March 1986. Although much of the province was brought to a standstill using peaceful protest, in a number of places the protests resulted in violence.
- The launching of a campaign of civil disobedience with measures including the shunning of British ministers, the refusal to set rates in Unionist-controlled councils and a boycott of Westminster.

At the same time Loyalist paramilitaries engaged in a campaign of violence and intimidation against the RUC who were seen as essential to the success of the Agreement. In addition, in November 1986 Ulster Resistance, a paramilitary organisation whose aim was the destruction of the Agreement, was formed.

RESULTS OF THE CAMPAIGN

By and large, however, these tactics failed. The Unionists gained a total of over 420,000 votes in the January 1986 by-elections; however, they lost one of their seats to the SDLP. The absence of fourteen Unionist MPs was not noticed at Westminster and since local councils had little power as it was, the refusal to use this power made little or no difference. By September 1987, when the Unionist leaders agreed to talk to British ministers again, it was clear that the campaign to destroy the Agreement had failed.

ACTIVITIES

1. Create a spider diagram illustrating the different ways in which the Unionist community demonstrated its opposition to the Anglo–Irish Agreement.
2. Taking each method of opposition in turn, indicate why it was a success or a failure.

The Cold War 1945–1991

A CLASH OF IDEOLOGIES? COMMUNISM VERSUS CAPITALISM BEFORE 1945

THE ORIGINS OF THE COLD WAR

WHAT YOU NEED TO KNOW

Although most historians date the official start of the Cold War to 1945, there are longer-term causes that you should be aware of.

The origins of the Cold War can be traced back to October 1917 when Lenin's communists seized power in Russia. This greatly worried countries like Britain and the USA as communism sought the destruction of their **capitalist** system.

Britain, France, Japan and the United States helped the communists' opponents in the civil war that followed the 1917 revolution. The communists won the war but they never forgot the fact that capitalist nations had tried to destroy them.

This mutual suspicion continued and deepened throughout the 1920s and 1930s. For example:

- Russia was not invited to the 1919 Paris Peace Conference.
- Russia was not allowed to join the League of Nations.
- It was not until 1924 that the British government officially recognised the communist regime as Russia's government. (America followed suit in 1933.)
- During the later 1930s Britain and France refused to form an alliance with Russia against Nazi Germany.

Joseph Stalin succeeded Lenin as leader of Russia (now the USSR or Soviet Union). He acted to protect the USSR from attack by the West.

- He began a series of Five-Year Plans to ensure that the Soviet economy would be ready to fight a war.
- He signed a non-aggression pact with the Nazis in August 1939. Stalin knew that Hitler wanted to destroy communism, but it suited him to delay the war for a while until the USSR was ready to fight.

ACTIVITIES

1 Create a timeline illustrating the key developments in the Cold War up to 1944.
2 Create a spider diagram illustrating the reasons why the USSR felt under threat from the capitalist nations.

FIGHTING A COMMON ENEMY

Stalin and the Allies joined forces when Germany invaded the USSR in June 1941. However, he remained suspicious of the West, claiming that they delayed D-Day until June 1944 to see if Germany and the USSR would wear each other out.

RENEWING DIVISION: THE EVENTS OF 1945

WHAT YOU NEED TO KNOW

East–West relations changed between the Yalta and Potsdam Conferences. You must be able to explain **why** relations deteriorated so much and what was agreed (and not agreed) at these meetings.

YALTA

In February 1945 Churchill, Roosevelt and Stalin (the Big Three) met at Yalta to discuss post-war Europe. Each leader had different aims:

- *Churchill* wanted to ensure the survival of the British Empire. He also saw the USSR as a danger to the West that had to be stopped.
- *Roosevelt* sought the creation of a free world that would be protected by the **United Nations** (UN), a new peace-keeping body.

He wanted the USSR to join the UN and was prepared to work with Stalin to ensure that this happened.
- *Stalin* sought the creation of a 'buffer' zone between Western Europe and the USSR as a way of protecting the USSR from further attack. To ensure that the countries making up this zone would be friendly towards Moscow, Stalin wanted them to be controlled by communist governments.

AGREEMENTS MADE AT YALTA

Despite these differences, it was agreed that:

- Germany and Berlin would be divided into four zones to be occupied by the armies of Britain, France, the USSR and America
- Germany would pay reparations
- the UN would be established
- the USSR would declare war on Japan three months after Hitler was defeated
- Poland would have new borders (although no agreement was reached on the makeup of Poland's government)
- Eastern Europe would come under the influence of the USSR. However, it was also agreed that there would be democratic elections in these countries.

POTSDAM

By the time the Big Three met again at Potsdam in July 1945, several important changes had taken place:

- The war in Europe had ended and Hitler was dead.
- Soviet troops were spread throughout Eastern Europe.
- Plans were being made to return most US troops home.
- Roosevelt had died and been replaced by Harry Truman. Truman was suspicious of Stalin's aims and his advisers were also urging him to take a harsh line against Stalin.
- Labour's Clement Attlee replaced Churchill as Britain's Prime Minister during the Potsdam Conference.
- American and British attitudes towards the USSR were hardening as they watched Germany being stripped of resources and saw **puppet governments** being set up in countries under Soviet control.

In addition, Stalin's fear of the West increased when he was told that the US had developed the atomic bomb, and would not share the technology.

POTSDAM DECISIONS

At Potsdam the following was agreed:

- How Germany was to be divided and occupied. Each power could take reparations from their own zone, although not so much as to endanger the lives of ordinary Germans. The USSR could also take some reparations from the British and US zones in return for supplying food, fuel and raw materials.
- How Austria was to be divided and occupied.
- Changes to Germany's border with Poland. This border was moved westward to the Oder and Neisse Rivers. All former German territory to the east of the new border became part of Poland. At the same time the USSR's border with Poland was also moved to the west.

The suspicions and tensions of Potsdam marked the first 'drop in temperature' of what would become the Cold War.

ACTIVITIES

1. Create a timeline illustrating the key developments in the Cold War in 1945.
2. Create a spider diagram illustrating the main decisions reached at Yalta.
3. Use the following headings to explain the changes that took place between Yalta and Potsdam:
   - Second World War
   - US leader
   - UK leader
4. Create a spider diagram illustrating the main decisions reached at Potsdam.

THE EXPANSION OF COMMUNISM IN EASTERN EUROPE

WHAT YOU NEED TO KNOW

The creation of the Iron Curtain and the Western response to it speedily resulted in the collapse of East–West relations. You will be expected to know **which** countries became communist and **how** they became communist.

USA–USSR SUSPICIONS

The world at the end of 1945 was very different than it had been just six years earlier.

- The USSR and the USA were both far stronger than any other nation.
- Each feared that the other wanted to spread their influence.
- Each believed that the other wanted to destroy them.

CHURCHILL'S FULTON SPEECH

It was Winston Churchill who most clearly expressed the West's suspicion. In a speech made in Fulton, Missouri in March 1946, Churchill condemned Stalin's attempts to control Eastern Europe. It was in this speech that the phrase '**Iron Curtain**' was first used.

Stalin reacted angrily to the speech. He argued that the way in which the USSR had suffered during the war made its protection from future invasion only natural.

THE EMERGENCE OF THE BUFFER ZONE

It was the communist take-over of Eastern European countries that made Churchill speak out so strongly. Between 1945 and 1947, elections in a number of states resulted in the selection of governments friendly to the USSR. The West suspected that the elections were rigged. Moscow denied this.

By 1947 the following countries were ruled by communists:

- Albania
- Bulgaria
- Hungary
- Poland
- Romania.

In addition, communists held power in Yugoslavia, although its leader, Tito, a wartime hero in his own country, was less inclined to do what Stalin told him. However, as far as the West was concerned, Yugoslavia was just another communist state.

THE STEPS TO COMMUNISM

Although the take-over of each country (apart from Yugoslavia) differed to some degree, certain trends were common to each:

- Soviet pressure to ensure that communists obtained key positions in the temporary governments set up after the war.
- Suggesting radical changes to help economic recovery. This helped gain the communists popularity.
- Controlling elections to ensure a communist victory.

By the end of 1947 only Czechoslovakia remained free from communist control in Eastern Europe.

HOW THESE EVENTS WERE INTERPRETED

Each side viewed these events differently, thus increasing tension.

- America's view was particularly influenced by George Kennan, a US diplomat based in Moscow. He argued that the two superpowers could never live in peace and recommended that the US act to contain the USSR's aggression in the future. As a result the policy of **containment** was born.
- The US failed to understand that the USSR was obsessed with her own security. By seeing everything that Moscow did as evidence of the communists' desire to control Europe, suspicion, fear and hostility were increased.

ACTIVITIES

1 Create a spider diagram showing how Europe had changed (from 1939) by 1945.

2 Create a spider diagram indicating which countries had become communist by 1948.

3 Use the following headings to explain the main steps that communists took to ensure control of Eastern European countries:
- Step 1
- Step 2
- Step 3

EVENTS IN GREECE

After the end of the Second World War the Allies had agreed to help train and equip the Greek army in its fight against communists. In March 1947 the British government announced that it could no longer afford to continue funding the Greek army. This worried Truman. He feared that if Greece became communist, so too would neighbouring countries and the oil-rich Middle East.

CONGRESS HELPS

Truman believed that communism would spread more easily if countries were poor. He thought that if economic recovery took place in such countries:

- communism would fail to take control
- these countries would be able to trade with America, helping its own economy.

Truman therefore went to **Congress** for help. He told it that the US would use military or economic means to stop countries becoming communist. This policy became known as the Truman Doctrine. Congress released $400 million, providing enough support and equipment to end the communist threat in Greece.

US Secretary of State, General George Marshall, visited Europe in April 1947 and saw that many countries were in danger of economic collapse and a communist take-over. He proposed an investment of $13.3 billion over a four-year period. The money would be offered to any country that opened its markets to Western goods and made its economic records available for inspection. The investment became known as the Marshall Plan or Marshall Aid.

Initially Congress was unconvinced; however, the communist take-over of Czechoslovakia in February 1948 changed its mind. Sixteen countries, particularly Britain and the Allied parts of Germany, benefited from the Marshall Plan.

REACTIONS TO THE MARSHALL PLAN

Stalin described the Marshall Plan as 'dollar diplomacy'. He argued that America would use it to gain influence over countries. He rejected the offer of finance and made sure that all the countries he controlled did the same by:

- Establishing the Communist Information Bureau (Cominform). This aimed to ensure communist nations worked together more closely and effectively.
- Setting up the Council for Mutual Economic Assistance (Comecon). It was a Soviet version of the Marshall Plan, which encouraged economic co-operation among Iron Curtain states.

IMPACT OF THE MARSHALL PLAN

The Marshall Plan played a vital part in the economic reconstruction of Europe. However, it might also be seen to have played a central part in the ongoing destruction of East–West relations. 1947 was the year in which the phrase 'cold war' was first used to describe the East–West relationship.

WHAT YOU NEED TO KNOW

The ways in which the USA reacted to the spread of communism is crucial information. Make sure you are also clear about Stalin's response.

ACTIVITIES

1. Create a timeline illustrating the key developments in the Cold War, 1947–48.
2. Analyse the Truman Doctrine using the following headings:
   - Background
   - Definition
   - Terms
   - Results
3. Analyse Marshall Aid using the following headings:
   - Aims
   - Terms
   - Congress' initial response
   - How and why this response changed
   - Impact of investment
   - Stalin's response
4. Explain the purpose of Cominform and Comecon.
5. Create a spider diagram illustrating both the positive and negative impacts of the Truman Doctrine and Marshall Aid.

CONFRONTATION AND CONTAINMENT

CAUSES OF THE BERLIN BLOCKADE

At Yalta and Potsdam it had been agreed that Germany would be divided into four zones, each to be administered separately by the British, Americans, Soviets and French. Berlin was also divided, but as it was located over 100 miles inside the Soviet zone, the Allies had to travel through the Soviet area to get to the city.

WHAT YOU NEED TO KNOW

You need to know **why** the blockade happened, **what** happened during it and **what** impact it had on East–West relations.

However, that was as far as agreement had gone since both sides had completely different opinions about Germany's future.

- The Western powers wanted Germany to recover so it could be both a barrier against the further spread of communism and a cornerstone of European economic recovery. Therefore, significant resources were invested in Germany including over $1,300 million of Marshall Aid.
- The USSR wanted Germany to remain weak as Germany had invaded it twice since 1914.

By 1948 the Western zones of Germany were on the road to economic recovery. The same could not be said of the Soviet zone as the USSR had removed significant levels of resources to compensate for war damage.

INTRODUCING A NEW CURRENCY

By June 1948 the American, British and French zones had been merged and the Allies decided to introduce a new currency – the *Deutschmark* – into the region. Stalin was not consulted about this decision and was unhappy about it as:

- He saw it as the first stage in the reconstruction of a Germany which would again threaten the USSR.
- This recovery would be obvious to the poor people of East Berlin who were living so close to their Western neighbours. This could cause problems as discontent at lower living standards in the communist zone might develop.

Therefore, on 24 June 1948, Stalin ordered the closure of all transport links with West Berlin.

THE BERLIN AIRLIFT

Although several options were open to the US, most had to be scrapped because of the risk of war. It was decided that airlifting supplies to West Berlin would be the best way of breaking the blockade. It was felt that Stalin was unlikely to shoot planes down, as that would be seen as an act of war.

For almost a year, therefore, up to 13,000 tons of supplies were flown in daily. For long periods the two million citizens of West Berlin had to endure severe rationing, yet by mid-1949 Stalin was forced to admit defeat and on 12 May the blockade was lifted. Over two million tons of supplies had been airlifted in; 101 men had died, mostly as a result of plane crashes, but war had been avoided and Berlin had been saved from communism.

RESULTS OF THE BERLIN BLOCKADE

The Berlin Blockade was a significant turning point in the Cold War:

- The policy of containment could be seen to have worked – communism had failed to spread into West Berlin.
- In April 1949, 12 Western nations set up the **North Atlantic Treaty Organization (NATO)** to ensure that the West could co-operate to prevent future Soviet aggression. NATO was based around the principle that an attack on one of its members would be considered as an attack on all.
- Although NATO was established as a defensive organisation, the Soviets saw it as an aggressive alliance. This opinion seemed to be confirmed when West Germany was allowed to join NATO in 1955. Again Moscow's fear of a strong Germany was revived. In response, the Warsaw Pact was established in May 1955. It was basically a communist version of NATO with all countries in the Soviet sphere of influence agreeing to defend each other if one was attacked. The Pact was dominated by the USSR, however.

ACTIVITIES

1. Create a timeline illustrating the key developments in the Cold War, 1948–55.
2. Analyse the different attitudes to Germany's future using the following headings:
   - Western attitudes
   - Stalin's attitude
3. Analyse the Berlin Blockade by writing a sentence about each of the following headings:
   - New currency
   - Living conditions
   - Stalin's response
   - US reaction
   - Details of airlift
   - Blockade end
4. Analyse the results of the Berlin Blockade using the headings of:
   - NATO
   - Warsaw Pact
   - Germany

- In May 1949 the **Federal** Republic of Germany (known as West Germany) was established. In October the USSR renamed its zone the German Democratic Republic (East Germany).

THE SPREAD OF COMMUNISM IN ASIA 1945–75 (I)

WHAT YOU NEED TO KNOW

The fall of China to communism was a massive development in the Cold War, turning it into a worldwide struggle. You need to understand in particular how the USA and USSR responded to the communist takeover.

CHINA

While communism seemed to have been contained in Europe, it was soon emerging elsewhere. Since the 1920s Chinese communists, led by Mao Zedong, had been fighting a civil war with Chiang Kai-shek's nationalist Kuomintang (KMT). They joined forces to fight the Japanese during the Second World War, but soon after conflict was renewed. Despite US support for the KMT, the communists were eventually victorious and on 1 October 1949, Mao Zedong announced the establishment of the People's Republic of China. Chiang Kai-shek fled to the nearby island of Formosa (later renamed Taiwan).

USSR'S REACTION TO THE COMMUNIST TAKE-OVER

The USSR was delighted that China had become communist and Stalin was determined to establish a link with his newly communist neighbour. Therefore, in 1950 a Treaty of Friendship was agreed; this committed the USSR to support China's economic, technological and military development.

USA'S REACTION TO THE COMMUNIST TAKE-OVER

The USA was very worried by these developments; China was a vast country with a massive population and huge resources; its fall to communists turned the Cold War into a worldwide struggle. The USA (wrongly) suspected that the fall of China was part of Stalin's plans to make the world communist. Truman's regime came under massive domestic criticism for its failure to stand up to the communists.

Since it regarded Mao Zedong as little more than Stalin's puppet, the US government:

- Refused to recognise the new regime as China's legitimate government.
- Tried its best to ignore communist China and continued to support Chiang Kai-shek's right to represent China in the UN.

Stalin's attempts to obtain the Chinese seat at the UN for the communists were rejected; in response the Soviet delegation to the UN staged a walkout.

ACTIVITY

1 Analyse the response to the communist take-over of China by completing the following table:

	USSR	USA
Reaction		
Steps taken		

THE THREAT TO ASIA

What did the communist take-over in China mean for Asia? Would China's neighbours follow suit? Would Japan be a target? The USA's fear of neighbouring countries becoming communist one after another became known as the **domino theory.** To stop this happening, containment would have to become a worldwide policy.

THE SPREAD OF COMMUNISM IN ASIA 1945–75 (II)

WHAT YOU NEED TO KNOW

Korea is where the Cold War became 'hot' for the first time. Make sure that you can explain why the Korean War started and how it developed in its early stages.

KOREA

In 1945 Korea was freed from Japanese control by Soviet troops who moved into the north of the country and by American soldiers who landed in the south. The country was **partitioned** along the 38th parallel until elections could be held and the country reunited.

THE EMERGENCE OF TWO STATES

Unfortunately the two superpowers could not agree about Korea's future:

- Moscow wanted it to become communist.
- Washington wanted it to become a capitalist democracy.

By the time both armies left in 1949, two separate governments had been set up:

- In the north a communist regime was set up under Kim Il Sung. The new state was called the Korean People's Democratic Republic but became known as North Korea.
- In the south a capitalist dictatorship was established, led by Syngman Rhee. Officially christened the Republic of Korea, more commonly it was called South Korea.

THE START OF THE WAR

Both states sought the reunification of the country and on 25 June 1950, North Korea invaded the south. Within days the capital Seoul had been captured. The US – believing that Stalin had encouraged the invasion – asked the UN to intervene. First the UN condemned the attack; then it began to put together a military force to stop the invasion.

UN RESPONSE

The USSR was unhappy but it was unable to use its **veto** to object to the UN's actions as it was boycotting the UN in protest at America's refusal to recognise China's new communist regime or to allow communist China to sit on the UN **Security Council**.

The UN force, which was mainly American and led by the American General Douglas MacArthur, landed at Inchon in September 1950. Before long it had pushed the North Korean forces back over the 38th parallel.

Crossing the 38th parallel meant that the UN force was exceeding its orders. However, MacArthur's plan (and Truman's) was to reunite Korea. This worried North Korea's neighbour China, which was afraid that the US would try to invade China and restore Chiang Kai-shek and his nationalists. As a result Mao Zedong issued a warning to the UN about the consequences of its actions.

ACTIVITIES

1. Create a timeline illustrating the background to and events of the Korean War up to 1950.
2. Analyse the Korean War by explaining the following headings:
   - Korea 1939–45
   - Korea 1945–49
   - Invasion
   - US reaction
   - USSR reaction
   - UN invasion

CHINA'S RESPONSE

China's fears seemed to be confirmed when MacArthur pushed on as far as the Yalu River, North Korea's border with China. In response, over 250,000 Chinese troops (called 'volunteers' rather than soldiers so that war would not have to be declared) invaded North Korea in November 1950 and pushed the UN forces back over the 38th parallel.

MacArthur now begged Truman to allow him to destroy Chinese communism; he even urged the use of the atomic bomb. Truman, however, had decided on containment and, fearing direct Soviet intervention, he refused to agree. In April 1951 he sacked MacArthur after the General had openly criticised the President's policies.

The war dragged on until the middle of 1951 when both sides dug in. It then took to the skies where US and USSR pilots (the latter dressed in Chinese uniforms and flying planes with Chinese markings) fought for a further two years. These dogfights were kept secret from the US population in case they demanded all-out war with the USSR.

WHAT YOU NEED TO KNOW

The war became much more dangerous once China became involved. Make sure you can explain **why** this happened, **how** the conflict then developed and **what** impact it had.

THE END OF THE WAR

Peace talks started in June 1951 but were unable to find an acceptable solution. In 1953 President Eisenhower succeeded Truman and Stalin died, eventually leaving Nikita Khrushchev in control. Both leaders sought peace and a ceasefire was agreed at Panmunjom in July 1953. Although a peace treaty was never signed, the agreement saw the creation of a permanent border – slightly north of the 38th parallel – and a demilitarised zone (DMZ) between the two states.

ACTIVITY

1. Create a timeline illustrating the events of the Korean War 1950–53.

RESULTS OF THE KOREAN WAR

- Over 2 million died.
- Containment had worked: communism did not spread into South Korea.
- The relationship between North and South Korea remained tense and bitter.
- US–Chinese relations deteriorated further.
- To prevent Japan falling to communism, America signed a peace treaty, ended military occupation and invested heavily in the Japanese economy.
- The US signed agreements with the Philippines, Australia and New Zealand, confirming its position as the protector of the region.
- NATO was changed from a mainly political association into a full-blown military alliance.

ACTIVITIES

2 Analyse the Korean War by explaining the following headings:
- UN campaign beyond 38th parallel
- China's reaction
- MacArthur and Truman
- Korea 1951–53
- Ceasefire

3 Create a spider diagram indicating the main results of the Korean War.

THE SPREAD OF COMMUNISM IN ASIA 1945–75 (III): THE VIETNAM WAR

WHAT YOU NEED TO KNOW

In many ways, Vietnam is as complicated as Korea. Again you need to be clear about the **background** to the conflict and the **reasons why** the USA got involved.

BACKGROUND: WAR WITH FRANCE

Since the nineteenth century Vietnam had been part of the French Empire. During the Second World War the Japanese replaced the French as occupiers but they soon found themselves under attack from the Vietminh, a nationalist army led by the communist Ho Chi Minh.

At the end of the war the Vietminh declared Vietnam independent. When the French tried to move back in, they were resisted by the Vietminh. Initially the US opposed French actions as **colonialism**, but by 1950 it began to provide support for the French. This was because it now saw the war as part of the ongoing struggle against communism.

The French suffered a humiliating defeat at Dien Bien Phu in 1954. This was followed by an armistice in which Vietnam was divided along the 17th parallel. The northern part would be under Vietminh control while the anti-communist Ngo Dinh Diem would control the South. It was agreed that after elections were held the country would be reunited.

The elections never took place as the South Vietnamese government and the US were afraid that the communists would win. The US was also afraid that if this happened, neighbouring countries would also fall to communism.

INCREASED US INVOLVEMENT

President Eisenhower provided money, weapons and military advisors for the South Vietnamese government. His successor, John F. Kennedy, increased the levels of aid. All this came at a time of increasing **guerrilla** attacks against the South's army by the National Liberation Front or Vietcong. It had been set up in 1960 to reunite the country under communist control and was supported by Ho Chi Minh.

Unfortunately for the US, Ngo Dinh Diem was an unpopular leader. His regime was brutal and corrupt and the government – made up of mostly Catholic landowners – was out of touch with the mainly Buddhist peasant population. The Vietcong gained more and more support and control. In November 1963 Diem was overthrown and assassinated by the Vietcong. Shortly after, Kennedy himself was killed; by then there were 16,000 US military advisors in Vietnam.

THE TONKIN RESOLUTION

In August 1964 the North Vietnamese attacked a US destroyer, *USS Maddox*, in the Gulf of Tonkin. In response, Congress passed the Tonkin Resolution, allowing President Lyndon B. Johnson to fight a war as he saw fit.

Over the next three years massive numbers of troops arrived in Vietnam and the US Air Force launched repeated bombing raids

ACTIVITIES

1 Create a timeline illustrating the background to the Vietnam War.

2 Analyse the background to and early stages of the Vietnam War by explaining the following headings:
- Vietnam before 1939
- Vietnam 1939–45
- Vietnam 1945–54
- Armistice
- No election?
- NLF and US involvement
- Ngo Dinh Diem

(Operation Rolling Thunder) against the Vietcong. The US used chemicals such as napalm (a petroleum jelly) and Agent Orange (which can damage the brain and the central nervous system) in their bombing raids. The former burned civilians indiscriminately; the latter cleared the forests of foliage. This enabled the Americans to see their enemy from the air; however it also destroyed the land and wounded countless civilians.

REASONS FOR THE USA'S DIFFICULTIES

With over 500,000 troops in Vietnam by 1968, the US should have easily defeated its enemy. However, the expected victory did not happen; indeed the opposite seemed to be the case. In many ways this was not surprising:

- The Vietnamese had already seen off foreign armies (French and Japanese).
- The US army was made up of many inexperienced soldiers (**conscripts**). Moreover, it was fighting an enemy which used guerrilla tactics, dressed in the same way as the Vietnamese peasantry and knew the country well.
- The Vietcong developed a vast network of underground tunnels to support their guerrilla campaign.
- The Vietnamese people had no reason to support the US forces, which seemed prepared to harass and kill civilians in their efforts to root out the Vietcong. The most notorious example of this was the My Lai massacre of March 1968 when nearly 350 villagers were massacred by a company of US troops. The platoon leader, Lieutenant William Calley, was imprisoned for life but later pardoned by President Richard M. Nixon.

WHAT YOU NEED TO KNOW

Why and **how** the USA increased its involvement, the **impact** of the war in Vietnam and in the USA, **how** it ended and **what** its results were are the key issues for you to gain an understanding of.

THE BEGINNING OF THE END

In January 1968 the Vietcong launched a massive counter-offensive (known as the Tet Offensive) against the US forces. Vietcong troops got as far as the South's capital, Saigon, before they were driven back. Although ultimately a failure militarily, the Tet Offensive made Americans feel that they could not win this war.

The same feelings were beginning to emerge back in the US. More and more Americans were being drafted (conscripted) and more and more were coming home in body bags. Complaints were made about the cost of the war. Students protested against the US government's policies. Many of those being called up burned their **draft cards**. Johnson himself became so unpopular that he decided not to run for re-election in 1968.

The demonstrations continued after Nixon became President; in one such protest the National Guard killed four students during a protest at Kent State University, Ohio. Even serving soldiers began to object about the job they had been sent to do.

Nixon was determined to remove the US from the Vietnam War, but he wanted to do it in a way that did not make America look as if it had lost. To this end he:

- Increased the levels of bombing against North Vietnam and its capital Hanoi.
- Ordered secret bombing raids against the neighbouring countries of Cambodia and Laos in 1970. This was because they were being used as supply routes by the Vietcong (the so-called Ho Chi Minh Trail). In total up to 10 million tons of bombs were dropped by the USA on Vietnam.
- Introduced the policy of Vietnamisation. By this US troops would be withdrawn and South Vietnamese forces would do the fighting.

PEACE TALKS

In 1973, after several years of negotiations, a peace treaty was signed in Paris. It allowed for the withdrawal of US forces and the return of US prisoners of war. It also allowed the Vietcong to remain in the South and put off a decision on the country's political future until a later date.

Nixon felt able to argue that he had achieved his aim of 'peace with honour' but by 1975 all of Vietnam was in the hands of the communists; American involvement seemed to have achieved very little at an immense cost.

RESULTS OF THE VIETNAM WAR

- There were huge military and civilian losses:

Country	Military dead	Military wounded	Civilian dead
North Vietnam	900,000	2,000,000	1,000,000
South Vietnam	250,000	600,000	
United States	58,132	300,000	

- Many US veterans suffered severe mental damage as a result of their experiences.
- Vietnam was devastated by the war – economically, socially and geographically.
- Cambodia and Laos also became communist; the policy of containment seemed to have failed.
- The US spent at least $120 billion on the war.
- The war proved that an enemy that used suitable tactics could humble the USA.

ACTIVITIES

1 Create a timeline illustrating the events of the Vietnam War after the Tonkin Resolution.

2 Analyse the Vietnam War by explaining the following headings:
- Tonkin Resolution
- US tactics
- Problems defeating Vietcong
- Tet Offensive and impact of war in US
- Nixon's tactics
- 'Peace with honour'

3 Create a spider diagram illustrating the results of the Vietnam War.

THE 1962 CUBAN MISSILE CRISIS

WHAT YOU NEED TO KNOW

The Cuban Missile Crisis was perhaps as close to a Third World War that the Cold War came. Try to identify the **reasons** for the fallout between the US and Cuba, **how** the USSR got involved and **what** Kennedy's options were.

For most of the twentieth century, Cuba – a small landmass just 90 miles off the Florida coast – had exported its main crop, sugar, to the US while American companies controlled most of the island's industry.

FIDEL CASTRO

Since 1959 Cuba had been led by Fidel Castro. Castro was a nationalist who wished to ensure Cuba's independence. Once in power he began to nationalise industries, many of which were US-owned. This upset the Americans and as US hostility to Cuba grew, trade between the two nations declined. Castro turned to the USSR for assistance and before long it had become Cuba's main trading partner. In 1961, Castro announced that he had become a communist.

THE BAY OF PIGS

In January 1961, John F. Kennedy became US President. Shortly after he took over, the **CIA** informed him that they were planning an invasion of Cuba with the assistance of 1,500 anti-Castro Cuban exiles. Kennedy approved the invasion but it went totally wrong. Bad military intelligence led the invaders to overestimate the amount of support that they would receive. The invasion – which became known as the Bay of Pigs disaster after the bay on which the invaders landed – made Kennedy look inexperienced and turned Castro into a hero in Cuba.

MISSILES ARRIVE

Castro was deeply concerned by US attempts to overthrow him and he turned to Moscow for assistance. This resulted, in August 1962, in the arrival of equipment needed to establish nuclear missile bases in Cuba. Such missiles would be able to reach most US cities and would provide a counterbalance to US missiles installed in countries such as Turkey.

The US intelligence services obtained convincing proof of the missile bases by 14 October 1962. They also revealed that Soviet ships were en route to Cuba with further supplies. Kennedy was determined that he would not be made look foolish again; he would stand firm against the USSR's threat.

THE MISSILE CRISIS

Throughout the crisis, ExComm, a committee of the **National Security Council**, advised Kennedy. ExComm considered a range of options available to the US including:

- an invasion of Cuba
- a **naval blockade** of Cuba
- air attacks on the missile bases
- a nuclear attack on Cuba
- allowing the missile bases to be erected.

Each of the options had good and bad points.

Eventually, on 22 October, Kennedy decided on a naval blockade. On the same day he revealed the unfolding crisis in a television broadcast. The remainder of the crisis played out as follows:

23 October	Moscow condemned US actions as piracy and argued that it was only helping Cuba to improve its defences.
24 October	Beginning of US naval blockade. Plans for an American invasion of Cuba drawn up. US Air Force planes began to fly over Cuba. Upon reaching the naval blockade, the Soviet ships were either stopped or turned away. Evidence from U2 spy planes suggested that the missile sites were nearing completion.
26 October	Shooting down of a U2 spy plane over Cuba. Kennedy received a telegram from Khrushchev, which stated that the USSR would remove the missiles if America agreed to end the blockade and undertook not to invade Cuba.
27 October	A second telegram arrived from Khrushchev. This stated that the USSR would only remove its missiles from Cuba if America removed its missiles from Turkey. A U2 spy plane violated Soviet airspace. Kennedy decided to ignore Khrushchev's second telegram and reply to the first. He agreed to remove the blockade and not invade Cuba in return for the removal of Soviet missiles. He added that if he did not receive a reply by 29 October Cuba would be invaded.
28 October	Khrushchev agreed to Kennedy's offer and the removal of the missiles began.

RESULTS OF THE CRISIS

In public it looked like a great victory for Kennedy; however, he had secretly agreed to remove the US missiles in Turkey. In reality this was not a great sacrifice as the missiles were old and out of date. Within six months the US missiles were gone.

Several valuable lessons were learnt during the Cuban Missile Crisis. In particular both sides agreed that such a confrontation should be avoided in the future. To assist with this a telephone hotline between Washington and Moscow was set up. They also agreed to begin talks designed to reduce the number of nuclear weapons each side had. As a result, the **Partial Test Ban Treaty** was signed in 1963.

ACTIVITY

Analyse the background to and early days of the Cuban Missile Crisis by writing a sentence about each of the following headings:

- Cuba before Castro
- Reasons for US hostility
- Cuba and USSR
- Castro and communism
- Bay of Pigs
- Missiles
- US options

WHAT YOU NEED TO KNOW

Make sure you can explain **how** the Crisis developed and **how** it ended. Finally you need to be able to assess **which** side won and **explain** the changes brought in after the Crisis.

ACTIVITIES

1 Explain the following:
- Khrushchev telegram I
- Khrushchev telegram II
- Kennedy telegram

2 Who won the Cuban Missile Crisis? Write about the following to help you with your answer:
- Reasons it was a US victory
- Reasons it was not a US victory
- Reasons it was a Soviet victory
- Reasons it was not a Soviet victory
- Reasons it was a Cuban victory
- Reasons it was not a Cuban victory

HUNGARY

THE USSR: A NEW LEADER AND NEW POLICIES

Stalin died in March 1953. For a while the USSR had a **collective leadership** but by 1955 Nikita Khrushchev had emerged as the country's new leader. Initially his policies suggested that there might be a thaw in the Cold War:

- In 1955 he visited Yugoslavia and apologised for Stalin's policies.
- In the same year he agreed to meet the leaders of the West; the first such meeting for over a decade.
- In February 1956 he delivered an historic speech – known as the Secret Speech. In it he denounced Stalin's policies and urged the development of 'peaceful co-existence' with non-communist nations.
- He introduced the policy of destalinisation which was aimed at ending the influence of the dead leader over the USSR.
- He ordered the dissolution of Cominform.
- He spoke of there being 'different roads to socialism'.

Khrushchev's Secret Speech was listened to with great interest behind the Iron Curtain. There, people decided that his unheard-of criticism must mean disapproval of Stalin's policies. They began to believe that a more relaxed system of government might emerge in their countries.

WHAT YOU NEED TO KNOW

It is essential that you can explain **why** the rising took place, and **how** the East and West responded to it.

THE EMERGENCE OF OPPOSITION

Resentment at a decade of communist rule emerged first in Poland in July 1956. Although Soviet tanks crushed the opposition, Khrushchev agreed to the appointment of a moderate communist, Wladyslaw Gomulka, as leader and to the introduction of a number of reforms. However, he insisted that Poland remain communist.

The biggest revolt emerged in Hungary in October 1956. Hungarians had much to be angry about; under communist rule their religion had been oppressed, their economy ruined and their freedoms crushed.

Events of the Hungarian Rebellion

23 October	Hungarian students took to the streets demanding reforms.
26 October	As unrest grew, Imre Nagy, a moderate communist, was appointed as leader in place of the hardline Matyas Rakosi.
1 November	Nagy announced that Hungary would hold free multi-party elections and would withdraw from the Warsaw Pact.
4 November	Over 6,000 Soviet tanks invaded Hungary. In the fierce fighting that followed, over 3,000 died and a quarter of a million fled westward. Nagy fled to the Yugoslav Embassy but was later arrested and executed. He was replaced by Janos Kadar and communist control was reasserted. At that stage some reforms were introduced.

The USSR's response indicated that it could not take the risk of a member of the Warsaw Pact leaving the organisation since it might result in:

- The opening of a gap in the Iron Curtain, leaving the USSR exposed to attack.
- The collapse of the Iron Curtain; if one country was allowed to break free then all the others might follow suit.

The Reaction of the West to the Rebellion

Throughout the crisis the people of Hungary had hoped for assistance from the West; however, nothing arrived except words of support. This was because:

- The West was preoccupied by the Suez Crisis. Britain and France had attacked Egypt over the decision by Egypt's President Nasser to nationalise the Suez Canal to provide funds for economic development.
- The US was in the middle of a Presidential election campaign.
- The West felt that it would be much more risky to confront the USSR in Eastern Europe, which it now accepted as a Soviet sphere of influence, than it was to confront communism in Asia.

More than anything, the events of 1956 suggested that Khrushchev's criticism of Stalin did not mean any change in the USSR's attitude to its defence.

ACTIVITIES

1. Create a timeline indicating the main events leading up to the Hungarian Uprising of 1956.
2. Analyse events in Hungary in 1956 under the following headings:
   - Reasons
   - Events
   - Results
   - Reactions

BERLIN: REASONS FOR DIFFICULTIES

WHAT YOU NEED TO KNOW

You need to be able to explain **why** Khrushchev was concerned, **how** he responded and **how** the West reacted.

In Berlin it was still possible for people to flee to the West through West Berlin. It is estimated that by 1962 over two million people – many highly skilled workers – had slipped through the Iron Curtain in this way. This worried the USSR:

- it meant a significant loss of workers
- it suggested people preferred to live under capitalism rather than communism.

Khrushchev was also concerned that West Berlin was being used as a 'listening post', enabling the West to gather information about activities behind the Iron Curtain.

KHRUSHCHEV'S RESPONSE

In 1958 Khrushchev attempted to force the West to leave Berlin by threatening to give East Germany control of access points to the city; however, he failed. In 1960 he attended a **summit** meeting, again hoping to persuade the West to leave but the meeting collapsed when he revealed that the USSR had shot down a U2 spy plane.

THE BERLIN WALL

The 1960 summit meeting increased tensions even further and a new wave of people fled, causing labour shortages in the east of the city. In August 1961 Khrushchev ordered the erection of a massive wall that made permanent the division of the city. Armed guards patrolled the wall and those attempting to cross it without permission ran the risk of being shot. The river of defections dwindled to a trickle. America protested but, unwilling to risk war, did nothing.

ACTIVITIES

1. Use the following headings to explain Khrushchev's concern about Berlin:
   - Manpower
   - Propaganda
   - Security
2. Use the following headings to explain the steps Khrushchev took to solve the problem of Berlin:
   - Action
   - Details
   - Result

THE 1968 CZECH RISING

WHAT YOU NEED TO KNOW

Make sure that you are able to explain **why** the reforms were introduced, **why** the Warsaw Pact countries were so concerned, **how** they acted, **how** their actions were justified and **how** the West responded.

THE USSR'S NEW LEADER

The USSR's Communist Party leadership removed Khrushchev in 1964. He was replaced by Leonid Brezhnev.

LEADERSHIP CHANGES IN CZECHOSLOVAKIA

In January 1968 Czechoslovakia's hardline leader Antonin Novotny was replaced by the more moderate Alexander Dubček. Dubček wanted Czechoslovakia to remain communist but he also knew that if that was to happen, reforms would have to be carried out. To achieve 'socialism with a human face' he introduced a series of political and economic reforms that included:

- freedom of speech and of the press
- less centralised economic control
- development of foreign trade
- removal of restrictions on travel abroad
- reduction in the powers of the secret police.

The new atmosphere produced by the reforms was christened the 'Prague Spring'.

Reactions to Dubček's Policies

Brezhnev feared that these reforms would be copied by other countries and would ultimately destroy the Iron Curtain. Poland and East Germany expressed similar fears. Dubček assured them of his commitment to socialism and guaranteed that Czechoslovakia would remain in the Warsaw Pact.

Despite Dubček's guarantees, Brezhnev ordered 400,000 troops into the country on 20 August 1968. He claimed that senior Czech communists had invited them in. Although it was officially a Warsaw Pact operation with troops from Bulgaria, East Germany, Hungary, Poland and the USSR, in reality it was mainly a Soviet force.

Response to Invasion

Dubček realised that resistance was pointless and urged Czechs to show their opposition through passive resistance. He was summoned to Moscow; on his return to Prague he announced that the 'Prague Spring' had ended. Dubček resigned a few months later and was replaced by the much more hard-line Gustav Husak.

ACTIVITIES

1 Analyse the background to the Czech Rising by writing about:
- The date of Dubček's appointment
- The reasons for Dubček's appointment
- Dubček's aims
- Dubček's policies
- The public reaction

2 Analyse the Warsaw Pact response to Dubček's policies under the headings of (i) Fear and (ii) Reaction.

3 Examine events following the Warsaw Pact invasion by commenting on the following headings:
- Czech reaction to invasion
- Dubček's fate
- Brezhnev Doctrine
- Response of the West

THE BREZHNEV DOCTRINE

Brezhnev justified his actions by arguing that it was the duty of communist countries to prevent another communist state from turning to capitalism. This became known as known as the Brezhnev Doctrine.

The West responded with little more than words of sympathy. America in particular was too caught up with the Vietnam War and accepted that there was no point in trying to intervene in events behind the Iron Curtain.

DÉTENTE

WHAT YOU NEED TO KNOW

Make sure that you understand **why** each country followed the policy of *détente*, **what** forms it took and **why** it finally ended.

ORIGINS

For part of the 1960s and most of the 1970s there was an improvement in East–West relations. This improvement became known as ***détente*** and resulted in the signing of a number of treaties and agreements.

Détente emerged for a number of reasons, including the strained relations that existed between the USSR and China by the late 1960s. America believed that if it could create better relations with China, this would put significant pressure on the USSR. The US also believed that both countries might help it end the Vietnam War by putting pressure on North Vietnam to negotiate a settlement.

BACKGROUND: SINO–SOVIET RELATIONS

Initially China and the USSR had got on well together; however, for a number of reasons relations then deteriorated:

- Both countries differed over the best methods of agricultural development.
- China believed the USSR wanted to dominate it.
- The USSR refused to share nuclear technology. China developed its own nuclear capability by 1964.
- China opposed the criticism of Stalin in Khrushchev's Secret Speech of 1956.
- The USSR supplied India with aircraft engines during a 1962 border dispute with China.
- China believed peaceful co-existence was a betrayal of communist ideas. They thought Khrushchev was being too soft with the West.
- China condemned the Soviet climb-down over Cuba.
- In 1969 a border dispute between the two powers resulted in the deaths of a number of military personnel.

By the late 1960s relations between the two states were at an all-time low.

REASONS FOR IMPROVING RELATIONS

America had been hostile to China since the communist victory in 1949. This suspicion had resulted in the formation of SEATO (the South East Asian Treaty Organization). This was a defensive organisation covering parts of Australasia and was similar in intent to NATO.

In turn China had been left feeling isolated by American policies such as the refusal to recognise its communist government and the refusal to allow it to sit on the Security Council of the UN. Nevertheless, by the late 1960s both sides began to realise that there could be benefits from an improved relationship. In particular:

- Economic advantages such as the opening of new markets to both countries and, in China's case, the possibility of the investment of capital and technological knowledge.
- Military benefits, in that the US wanted China to put pressure on North Vietnam to negotiate an end to the Vietnam War. At the same time China saw the USA as a possible ally against an increasingly powerful USSR.
- Diplomatic benefits that meant each country could use the other in their ongoing power struggles with the USSR.

In 1971 the US table tennis team was invited to visit China. This was followed by China's entry into the UN in 1971 and President Nixon's visit to China in February 1972. In the same year both countries signed a Friendship Treaty. The US finally granted China full diplomatic recognition in 1978.

THE IMPACT ON THE USSR

The USSR was concerned about the improvement in US–Chinese relations. Moscow's desire to keep China isolated was one of its main reasons for wanting to improve relations with the US, but there were other issues for both sides, including:

- The realisation that they had come too close to nuclear war in the 1960s and that new understandings needed to be reached.
- The need to cut back on military spending due to the fact that both countries were facing severe economic problems.
- Washington needed new export markets and Moscow badly needed foreign supplies of grain as her grain harvest had failed in 1972.

ACTIVITIES

1. Create a timeline to illustrate the history of *détente*.
2. Create a spider diagram to explain the reasons for the deterioration in Sino–Soviet relations.
3. Use the following headings to explain the benefits China and the US saw in improving relations:
   - Economic
   - Military
   - Diplomatic

DÉTENTE: THE KEY AGREEMENTS

A series of summit meetings were held between the USSR and USA at which the following key agreements were made:

Date	Name of agreement	Key details	Results
1972	Strategic Arms Limitation Talks (SALT I)	Limited the number of certain types of weapons.	Only certain types of weaponry were included; many more powerful missiles were left out.
1975	Helsinki Agreement	Acceptance of existing borders in Europe by USA. Agreement to improve human rights by USSR.	Human rights did not really improve behind the Iron Curtain.
1979	SALT II	Further limitations on weaponry.	Never approved by the US **Congress** because of the Soviet invasion of Afghanistan in December 1979.

ACTIVITIES

4 Use the following headings to explain the reasons why the USSR and the US wanted to improve relations with each other:
- China
- War
- Spending
- Exports

5 Analyse SALT I, the Helsinki Agreement and SALT II using the following headings:
- Strengths
- Weaknesses

CONCLUSIONS

While *détente* was far from perfect, issues that had previously caused tension – such as the division of Germany – ceased to be as contentious. This was because *détente* emerged in the relationship between West Germany, East Germany and the USSR (known as *Ostpolitik*). The USSR recognised West Germany as a country and permitted some movement of relatives from West to East Berlin. In addition, the USSR benefited significantly from Western grain imports. However, relationships were thrown back into the deep freeze with the Soviet invasion of Afghanistan in 1979. Moscow's aim was to install a government loyal to the USSR.

THE COLLAPSE OF COMMUNISM

WHAT YOU NEED TO KNOW

Examiners will expect you to be able to explain **why** US–USSR relationships deteriorated so badly and then **how** they improved so much within such a short period of time.

'STAR WARS'

In 1981 the passionately anti-communist Ronald Reagan became US President. Under Reagan a new range of up-to-date missiles was introduced. A significant number of these missiles were based in Europe.

Reagan supported the development of the Strategic Defence Initiative (SDI), a laser defence system that would effectively create a shield around the USA, which could not be penetrated by Soviet missiles. Perhaps not surprisingly it was nicknamed 'Star Wars'.

ECONOMIC PROBLEMS

'Star Wars' cost billions of dollars and before long the US economy was in difficulty. However, the situation was even worse in the USSR. As Moscow tried to keep up with US technological advances, the already crumbling Soviet economy came close to total collapse. Both countries urgently needed to reduce costs.

The state of the Soviet economy particularly concerned Mikhail Gorbachev, who took over as leader of the USSR in March 1985. Gorbachev knew that the USSR could not afford to spend money in a vain attempt to keep up with US defence spending because:

- Living standards in the USSR were appallingly low.
- Due to corruption within the Communist Party, money was being wasted.
- Millions were on the verge of starvation because of the poor performance of the country's agricultural sector.
- Most main industries were in dire need of modernisation.
- Technologically the USSR was decades behind the West.
- The war in Afghanistan was draining billions from the economy.

ACTIVITIES

1 Create a timeline illustrating the main developments in US–USSR relations, 1980–91.

2 Analyse the US approach to the Cold War in the early 1980s by writing a sentence about:
- Reagan and the USSR
- New missiles
- 'Star Wars'

GORBACHEV'S FOREIGN POLICY

Gorbachev knew that economic reform would have to be preceded by huge cuts in defence spending. Such cuts would require a better relationship with the West.

In March 1985, therefore, Gorbachev announced the end of the Brezhnev Doctrine. The thinking behind this was simple: his decision to end the Cold War meant that the Eastern European buffer zone was no longer needed. To show that he meant what he said, Gorbachev began to withdraw Soviet troops from Eastern Europe.

ARMS LIMITATION TALKS

In 1987 Reagan and Gorbachev agreed an Intermediate Nuclear Forces (INF) Treaty. This ensured the removal of nearly 4,000 nuclear warheads and the halting of the 'Star Wars' programme. In 1988 Gorbachev announced the withdrawal of Soviet forces from Afghanistan and a huge reduction in the size of the Soviet armed forces. Troops were also withdrawn from other Iron Curtain countries.

Under Reagan's successor, George H. Bush (elected in November 1988), the changes continued. Bush met Gorbachev in Malta in 1989 and both leaders declared that the Cold War was over. In July 1991 the Warsaw Pact was dissolved.

ACTIVITIES

3 Create a spider diagram illustrating the problems facing the Soviet economy at this time.

4 Analyse Gorbachev's foreign policy using the following headings:
- Reason for changing foreign policy
- Changes introduced
- Results

GLASNOST AND *PERESTROIKA*

WHAT YOU NEED TO KNOW

You need to understand **what** reforms Gorbachev brought in, **why** he did so and **what** their impact was in the different countries across the region. Be aware also of **what** was going on in China and **how** communism finally came to an end in the USSR.

REFORM

Gorbachev knew that the USSR had to change politically and economically, if it was to survive. The first step was to end the arms race so that money could be invested in the Soviet economy. However, Gorbachev also encouraged Russians to offer constructive criticism of the communist system.

Gorbachev stated that his reforms would revolve around the ideas of *perestroika* and *glasnost*:

- *Perestroika*: restructuring of the Soviet economy through the introduction of more Western-style policies.
- *Glasnost*: openness. In other words there would be freedom to debate, freedom for the media, freedom from government control.

REACTIONS BEHIND THE IRON CURTAIN

The people of the other Iron Curtain countries watched the changes in the USSR with great interest. Gorbachev's policies meant that similar freedoms were now within their own grasp. 1989 was the year in which most countries broke free.

THE OPENING OF THE IRON CURTAIN

In each country the search for freedom took a slightly different path:

Country	Key dates	Events
East Germany	1989 1990	October: Gorbachev visited East Berlin and encouraged people to push for democracy. October: East Germany's leader, Erich Honecker resigned. November: The Berlin Wall was opened. October: Germany was reunified.
Bulgaria	1989	February: Free trade unions established. November: Communist leadership resigned.

Country	Key dates	Events
Romania	1989	December: After authorising the killings of large numbers of people protesting for food, dictator Nicolae Ceaușescu fled. Later he was executed by the army. Romania was the only country where the collapse of **communism** was accompanied by significant levels of violence.
Poland	1980 1981 1989	Solidarity set up as the first free trade union within the Iron Curtain. It soon had nine million members. Government recognised Solidarity. Under pressure from Moscow, Poland's leader, General Jaruzelski, declared martial law. Solidarity was declared illegal but continued to exist underground. April: Solidarity was legalised again after a wave of strikes. Workers were granted the right to strike. June: Solidarity won Poland's elections. August: A non-communist government was installed. December: Lech Walesa became President of Poland.
Czechoslovakia	1989 1993	May: Huge protest rallies were organised to demand change. November: After some initial resistance the communist regime was overthrown with almost no loss of life. This became known as the 'Velvet Revolution'. December: The Chairman of the newly elected **federal** parliament was Alexander Dubček. Playwright Vaclav Havel became President. Czechoslovakia split into Czech Republic and Slovakia.
Hungary	1988 1989	Hardline leader Janos Kadar was sacked and Imre Nagy was given a state funeral. January: Opposition parties were allowed. March: Demonstrations were held against Soviet troops. May: Fences cutting off the border with Austria were removed. As a result many East Germans went through Hungary and Austria into West Germany. October: A non-communist government was set up.
Baltic States	1990 1991	Initially even Gorbachev resisted the demands of Latvia and Lithuania for freedom, as he feared that it would encourage the other republics that made up the USSR to seek the same. Estonia, Latvia and Lithuania declared their independence.
Yugoslavia	1980 1990 1991–95	Death of Tito. Emergence of four different regimes within Yugoslavia. A series of wars were fought among the various ethnic groups in the region.

FREEDOM FOR ALL?

In China things were very different. A wave of student demonstrations between April and June 1989 ended in disaster in Beijing's Tiananmen Square when government forces crushed the opposition movement.

CRISIS IN RUSSIA

Nor was all well in Moscow; the economy was still in crisis and society seemed to be in a state of collapse. The USSR was divided between those who thought there had been too much change and those who felt that there had not been enough. One of the latter was Boris Yeltsin who was elected leader of Russia in 1990. Russia was the largest of the different Republics that together made up the USSR.

In August 1991 an attempt was made to overthrow Gorbachev. The **coup** was defeated by loyal troops and Gorbachev was soon reinstated. Yet within four months the Communist Party had been outlawed in Russia and the USSR had ceased to exist: all fifteen member republics had declared their independence. Gorbachev resigned as President of the USSR on Christmas Day 1991.

ACTIVITIES

1. Create a timeline indicating the changes that took place behind the Iron Curtain, 1980–91.
2. Define *glasnost* and *perestroika*.
3. Create a spider diagram illustrating the Iron Curtain countries that achieved their freedom from communist control, along with the date on which they achieved it.
4. Analyse the collapse of communism in the USSR by explaining the following headings:
   - Condition of country
   - Attitudes to reform
   - 1991 coup
   - End of communism
   - Gorbachev

GLOSSARY

Abdicate	To give up the position of king or queen.
Abdication crisis	The time in 1936 when Britain's King Edward VIII abdicated so that he could marry a divorced American, Wallis Simpson.
Alliance Party of Northern Ireland (APNI)	Launched in April 1970 and led by Oliver Napier. Although broadly unionist in its ideas, the Alliance Party opened its doors to supporters from all denominations. It was hoping to achieve the parts of Prime Minister Terence O'Neill's promises of reform not yet introduced.
Allies/Allied Forces	The name given to Britain, France, the USA and Russia during the First and Second World Wars.
Anschluss	Union between Austria and Germany (German).
Anti-Semitism	Anti-Jewish ideas.
Appeasement	The policy of making concessions to an opponent in the hope that they will stop making demands.
Apprentice Boys	A Loyalist club set up to remember the group of apprentices who closed the gates of Derry/Londonderry against the armies of King James II in 1689.
Ard Fheis	Annual Party Conference (Irish).
Armistice	A truce or ceasefire.
Aryan	The master race in Nazi Germany, made up of individuals of northern European descent and excluding those of a Semitic background.
Autarky	Economic self-sufficiency – not having to rely on other countries for supplies.
Backbencher	An MP who is a member of the government party but who does not have a job in the government.
Barrage balloon	A large balloon attached to steel cables which are then securely attached to the ground. The height of the balloons is adjustable. The balloons forced enemy aircraft to fly higher (to avoid contact with the cables) thus limiting their accuracy when bombing targets.
Barter economy	When goods rather than money are given in exchange for some service or other.
Boycott	To cut off connections with a person, group or organisation.
British Commonwealth	An association of countries that were formerly colonies of Great Britain.
B Specials	Part of the Ulster Special Constabulary (see below).
By-election	A special election held between general elections to replace an MP who has died or resigned.
Capitalist	An economic system (or a person supporting it) which believes in private ownership and the making of profits.
Censorship	Prevention of the publication of unwanted viewpoints.
Chancellor	Prime Minister of Germany.
CIA	Central Intelligence Agency. A US government body set up in 1947 to collect information on foreign groups and governments.
Civil disobedience	Protesting peacefully against alleged injustice.
Civil service/servants	A government's administrative support.
Civil war	A war between members of the same nation.
Coalition	A government or agreement made up of different political parties or countries.
Collective leadership	Leadership of a country by more than one person.
Colonialism	The belief that rich countries should control or rule poorer countries.
Communism/Communist(s)	The ideas of Karl Marx who supported a system of rule where industries were run by the government for the good of the people.
Concentration camps	Detention camp for political prisoners.
Concordat	Agreement between a state and the Catholic Church.

Congress	The US parliament.
Conscription/conscripts	Compulsory military service and those who join the armed forces.
Constitution	A document setting out the rules by which a country is to be run.
Constitutional monarchy	A political system where power is shared between a monarch and a parliament.
Containment	A policy introduced by the USA to stop the spread of communism.
Coup	Usually a violent overthrow of a government by military force.
Cumann na nGaedheal	The pro-Treaty party established in the aftermath of the split in Sinn Fein over the 1921 Treaty. It was the government of Ireland from 1922–1932. (Irish, meaning 'Society of the Gaels'.)
Dáil Éireann	The lower house of the Irish Parliament. (Irish, meaning 'Assembly of Ireland'.)
Demilitarise	To ensure an area does not have a military presence.
Democracy	A system whereby the people freely elect a government on a regular basis.
Democratic Unionist Party (DUP)	Originally known as the Protestant Unionist Party, the Democratic Unionist Party emerged in September 1971. Led by Reverend Ian Paisley, its aim was to defend the constitution of Northern Ireland while also reforming its economy and society.
Détente	The period from the late 1960s until the late 1970s when relations between the USA and USSR seemed to ease a little (from the French word for relaxation).
Devolved/Devolution	A political system where local parliaments are given some powers by the central parliament.
Diktat	A dictated peace (German).
Direct Rule	The system by which Northern Ireland was ruled directly from Westminster and not by its own local parliament.
Discrimination	Acting in an unfair way towards people of a different race or religion.
Dominion	A self-governing colony.
Domino theory	The fear that once one country fell to communism, neighbouring countries would do likewise.
Draft card(s)	A document requiring US citizens to undertake military service.
Duties	A type of tax.
Fascism	A set of political ideas developed by Benito Mussolini in Italy. Based on extreme nationalist ideas.
Federal	A political system with central and local parliaments, each with their own areas of responsibility.
General election	An election held for all the seats in a parliament.
Gerrymandering	The practice of drawing electoral boundaries in a way that benefits one particular group at the expense of another.
Governor General	Representative of the monarch in a dominion.
Guerrilla war	A conflict where one side tends to use hit and run tactics against a superior enemy (Spanish, meaning 'little war').
Hossbach Memorandum	The record of a 1937 meeting where Hitler explained his ideas about Germany's foreign policy.
Hyperinflation	Massive increases in prices.
Imperialism	The idea of a country having colonies.
Indoctrination	Process of imposing beliefs (political/racial) on an individual or group of people.
Inflation	Increase in prices.
Intern/Interned/Internment	Imprisonment without trial.
Irish Dimension	The idea that the Irish government should have some input into how Northern Ireland is governed.
Irish Republican Army (IRA)	A republican paramilitary group which was determined to create the Irish Republic as proclaimed in the 1916 Easter Rising.
Iron Curtain	A phrase used by Winston Churchill to explain how Europe had been divided between capitalism and communism.

Jehovah's Witness	A branch of Christianity founded in the US in the late nineteenth century.
Judiciary	The system of judges and courts.
Kaiser	Emperor of Germany (1871–1918).
League of Nations	A body established by the Paris Peace Settlement in 1919 in an attempt to provide a place where leaders could talk together and so avoid wars.
Left wing	Those who want sweeping political and economic changes.
Luftwaffe	The German Air Force.
Lundy	A term of insult within unionism, meaning that the person so-called is a traitor. Lieutenant Colonel Robert Lundy was the Governor of Derry/Londonderry during the siege of 1688–9. Rather than lead the defence of Derry/Londonderry against the forces of King James II, Lundy recommended surrender.
Lutheran (Church)	The main Protestant Church in Germany.
Manifesto	A political party's policies for running the country (published before an election).
Marxism/Marxist	The ideas of Karl Marx (see Communism).
Moderator	The leader of a church (usually Presbyterian).
National Security Council	A group which advises the US President on foreign policy issues.
Nationalise/Nationalisation	To bring under the ownership/control of the nation.
Nationalist	A person who seeks to protect the interests of a particular nation.
Naval blockade	The use of ships to prevent access by sea to an area/country.
Nazism	The ideology of National Socialist German Workers' Party. Based on extreme nationalist ideas.
New Ireland Forum	An attempt by the Irish Government to get all Irish political parties to agree a solution to the Northern Ireland problem. The Forum met from 1983–4; all suggested solutions were rejected by the British Government.
North Atlantic Treaty Organization (NATO)	Established in 1949, NATO is a military alliance initially set up to oppose the spread of communism/Soviet aggression.
No-go area(s)	Area of Northern Ireland that were policed by republican paramilitaries and which were not accessible to the RUC or British Army.
Official opposition	The second largest party in a parliament.
Ombudsman	An official who deals with complaints from the public.
Paris Peace Conference	The name given to a series of meetings held during the first part of 1919 involving the leaders of the victorious Allied powers (Britain, France, Italy, Japan and the United States). Their purpose was to draw up a series of peace treaties with the defeated powers (Austria, Bulgaria, Hungary, Germany and Turkey).
Paris Peace Settlement	The name given to a number of treaties drawn up at the end of the First World War at the Paris Peace Conference.
Partial Test Ban Treaty	Signed in 1963, this international agreement is a treaty outlawing all test detonations of nuclear weapons except underground.
Partition/Partitioning	The artificial division of a country.
Passive resistance	To oppose a group without using violence.
Planter	An individual (or his/her descendant) who took part in the colonisation of Ireland in the 1600–1700s.
Plebiscite	A type of referendum. A special vote where all the people of a country decide on a particular issue.
Points system	A system for determining council house allocation. A certain number of points were needed to gain a house and points were awarded for a variety of reasons.
Privy Council	Part of the British judicial system.
Propaganda	Political advertising.
Proportional Representation	A system of voting designed to create a result more in line with the way in which people voted.

Puppet government	A government that is under the control or influence of another state.
Radar	A system of using radio pulses to detect the location of aircraft and other objects.
Rates	A payment made by householders to their local council.
Red Army	The national army in the USSR or an army formed by a communist group.
Reichstag	The German parliament.
Reparations	The fine placed on Germany at the end of the First World War.
Republic	A form of government with no monarch.
Republican	Believer in a republic.
Reserved occupations	Job from which an individual will not be taken to serve in the armed forces.
Right wing	Those opposed to sweeping political and economic changes.
RTE	*Raidió Teilifís Éireann*, the Irish television service.
Secretariat	A group of civil servants supporting the work of the Anglo–Irish Agreement.
Secretary of State	A politician who is in charge of a government department and who is usually a member of the Cabinet. In the US the term refers specifically to the Foreign Minister.
Sectarian	To think or act in a way that discriminates against those of another religious group.
Security Council (UN)	One of the main sections of the United Nations, the Security Council is involved with peace-keeping activities and the authorisation of military action.
Social Democratic and Labour Party (SDLP)	Established in August 1970 and led by West Belfast MP Gerry Fitt, the SDLP was moderately left wing on social and economic issues. At the same time the party sought political reforms within Northern Ireland and the eventual re-unification of Ireland. The SDLP immediately became the main opposition party in Stormont, replacing the old Nationalist Party which had been led by Eddie McAteer.
Special Category Status	The recognition that those convicted of crimes connected with 'the Troubles' had acted for political and not criminal reasons.
Statute of Westminster	A law passed by the British Parliament in 1931 which stated that dominions were independent countries that could leave the Commonwealth without Britain's permission.
Stormont	The name given to the Northern Ireland Parliament building opened in 1932.
Subsistence	When farmers try to grow enough to feed themselves and their families.
Summit	A meeting between leaders of different countries.
Swastika	An ancient symbol that was adopted by the Nazis as their party emblem.
Taoiseach	The prime minister of the Republic of Ireland (Irish, meaning 'chieftain').
Tariff	A tax on imports or exports.
TD	Member of Dáil Éireann (Irish – *Teachta Dála* – Deputy to the Dáil).
The 'Troubles'	The name given to the period of violence in Northern Ireland that began in the late 1960s.
Trade deficit	When a country spends more money on importing goods than it makes from exporting goods.
Tribunal	A body set up to reach a decision on a particular issue.
Ulster Special Constabulary	A (mainly Protestant) reserve police force set up in late 1920.
Ulster Volunteer Force (UVF)	A paramilitary group originally set up in 1912 to oppose the introduction of Home Rule to Ireland.
Unionist	A person who wishes the political union between Great Britain and Northern Ireland to continue.

United Nations (UN)	An international peace-keeping organisation set up in 1945 to replace the League of Nations.
United Ulster Unionist Council (UUUC)	An anti-power-sharing umbrella grouping comprising of the Official Unionists, the DUP and the Vanguard Unionist Progressive Party, set up by William Craig to oppose power-sharing.
Veto	The right or ability to prevent or forbid an action or decision taking place.
Victoria Cross	Britain's highest military award, given for valour.
Wall Street Crash	The name given to the collapse of the US stock exchange in October 1929. This collapse had a huge impart not, only on the American economy, but on economies across the world.
Welfare State	A system where the government provides educational and health facilities for the people of a nation.